soft skills
for STRONG
LEADERS

soft skills *for* STRONG LEADERS
TEN STEPS TO MANAGEMENT SUCCESS

Helen Isacke

Copyright © Helen Isacke 2013

Published by New Generation Publishing in 2013
www.newgeneration-publishing.com

First Edition

The author asserts the moral right under the Copyright, Designs and Patents Act 1988 to be identified as the author of this work.

All Rights reserved. No part of this publication may be reproduced, stored in a retrieval system or transmitted, in any form or by any means without the prior consent of the author, nor be otherwise circulated in any form of binding or cover other than that which it is published and without a similar condition being imposed on the subsequent purchaser.

ISBN: 978-1-909878-82-2

Cover and text design by Emily Isacke
www.isacke.com

Cartoons by Roger Leboff
www.rogerleboff.com

This book is dedicated to my
beautiful daughters, Emily and Chloe,
who inspire me daily.

CONTENTS

Introduction 13

Part One: Preparing for Leadership

    Chapter One – Setting the Foundations
1. Soft Skills for Strong Leaders 22
2. Emotional Intelligence 24
3. Authentic Leadership 28
4. Leadership Values 29
5. A Leading Personality 38

    Chapter Two – Managing your Mindset
1. Self-Esteem and Confidence 44
2. Managing your Mindset 52
3. Limiting Beliefs 55
4. Setting your Intentions 60

    Chapter Three – Developing your Personal Brand
1. Your Personal Brand 68
2. Communicating your Brand 74
3. Grooming 77
4. Networking 79

Part Two: Your First 100 Days

    Chapter Four – Engaging your New Team
1. Your New Team 90
2. Setting a Clear Direction 95
3. Engaging your Team 100

    Chapter Five – Setting Expectations
1. Managing Expectations 108
2. What is Expected of You? 111
3. Clarify your own Expectations 115
4. Values and Beliefs 117
5. Unrealistic Expectations 123

Chapter Six – Managing Relationships
    1. The Blocks to Better Relationships   132
    2. FIRO Theory   136
    3. Representational Systems   142
    4. Rapport   145
    5. Listening Skills   149
    6. Managing your Stakeholders   152

Part Three: Day-to-Day Challenges
Chapter Seven – Exploring Emotions
    1. Unhelpful Emotions   161
    2. Harnessing Positive Emotions   169
    3. Stress   172
    4. Emotional Resilience   175
    5. Managing other People's Emotions   180
Chapter Eight – Handling Difficult Situations
    1. Difficult Meetings   188
    2. Difficult Conversations   192
    3. Handling Conflict   198
    4. Problem Solving   201
    5. Managing Change   206
Chapter Nine – Managing Time
    1. Prioritising   214
    2. Goal Setting   217
    3. Procrastination   218
    4. Perfectionism   219
    5. Interruptions   221
    6. Delegation   225
    7. Meetings   228
    8. Just say 'No'   229
    9. Getting Organised   231
    10. Motivation   232

Chapter Ten – Getting a Balance
- 1. Work Life Balance — 240
- 2. Personal Relationships — 244
- 3. Time for You — 247
- 4. Looking after your Body — 250

Afterword	255
Exercises	256
Top Tips	259
Recommended Reading	261
Acknowledgements	263
About the Author	264
Index	266

Introduction

At a workshop recently I introduced myself using my carefully crafted 'pitch'. I listed some of the reasons why new managers and leaders fail to make a positive impact; problems such as being too busy to delegate, avoiding difficult conversations, and the inability to influence effectively. I followed this by explaining how coaching can help address each of these, and much more. One of my fellow delegates came to me at the coffee break and said, "I wish I'd met you when I took on my first management role", reflecting on how he could relate to each of the issues I had mentioned. He continued to tell me that he had been prematurely promoted to a senior position, and had just about managed to keep his head above water, until he was made redundant a few years later. During his time as a senior leader, he was placed under immense pressure to deliver results, yet was offered little by way of support or personal development. There wasn't the time or the budget available. Yet once he was in the redundancy pool, he was offered £12,000 worth of outplacement support!

Promotion is generally awarded to those who can demonstrate good technical ability, yet being good technically doesn't automatically translate into being an effective leader. In addition to experience, knowledge and technical skills, strong leaders today also need to possess, and be able to demonstrate, soft skills.

Soft skills define who a leader is, rather than what he, or she, can achieve. They are the personal characteristics and attributes that underpin emotional intelligence; the ability to influence, communicate, motivate and inspire. It is the lack of these soft skills, and the lack of emotional intelligence that can de-rail the most technically knowledgeable leader. It is a well-known saying that people don't leave organisations, they leave their managers, and it is most often these managers who lack the essential man-management skills.

Investing in new leaders

Over the years, I've heard countless stories about leaders who have been 'let go' or moved sideways, because they are not delivering results, with the 'letting go' part costing the organisation hundreds of thousands of pounds. Why is it acceptable to invest heavily in the recruitment process for leaders, and then just leave them to get on with it? There is a large blind spot when it comes to investing in a new manager or leader, in those vital first few months – and beyond – when their performance is being closely judged. New leaders do not have the luxury of a honeymoon period to settle in, and have a limited time frame to prove that they are up to the job. Surely it makes sense to prepare and support them through this crucial transitional phase?

Changing the perception of coaching

In my experience, leaders tend to look for a coach when they are stuck, and don't know where else to turn. I have worked with many leaders who source their own personal coach, because they don't want their CEO or boss to view them as weak for seeking external support. Equally, it is not unusual to receive a call from an HR manager looking for an external coach to 'fix' a leader who is perceived to be struggling.

Individuals, who are moving from being one of the team, to leading and motivating a team, with demands from above and from below, require a different skill-set. A more robust method of enhancing these skills is needed, to help new leaders create high-performing teams, and deliver results.

Training tends to be the traditional approach for skills development, and yet the powerful personal development tool that coaching offers, in many organisations, is still misunderstood and underutilised. Training imparts generic information to a group of people, whereas coaching helps an individual or small team to develop specific leadership attitudes and behaviours, working towards defined business-related outcomes. Coaching doesn't replace training, but complements it.

It is time to change the perception of what coaching is, and demonstrate how it can be used in a pro-active way to prepare and support leaders in transition. Surely prevention is better – and more cost effective – than cure?

My mission is to make coaching as accessible and as acceptable as training is for leadership development.

About this book

I have written this book for aspiring and newly-appointed managers and leaders who are keen to develop their authentic leadership skills and attitudes, but might not - yet - have access to their own leadership or performance coach.

There are many books about leadership, so what makes this one different to the rest? It is written based ten years' practical experience of coaching managers and leaders. Many of these individuals had been on management training programmes, but they still weren't getting the results they desired. Coaching helped to fill the gaps, and addressed challenges that were not covered during training.

There are common issues which often prevent a leader performing to the best of their ability, and clients often remark to me, at some stage in the coaching process, 'I wish I had done this (coaching) years ago'. This tells me there is a need to prepare new leaders at a different level, beyond the usual management and leadership training programmes. This level is deeper and more personal, focusing on the soft skills needed to become a strong and effective leader. Coaching seems to reach the parts that many traditional training programmes don't touch.

In writing this book, I reviewed the issues that clients brought to their coaching sessions over the years, and grouped together the most common topics and themes. In doing so, I noticed that some chapters were more relevant to aspiring leaders, others to those in their first 100 days, and the rest to ongoing, day-to-day challenges.

Each chapter contains real-life case studies to illustrate how the theories have worked in practice. Scattered throughout the book, are questions which I might ask clients in a coaching session. They will facilitate your thinking, and can help develop the requisite soft skills, approaches and attitudes for leadership.

Pause and reflect

To get the most from the book, please take time to pause and reflect upon your responses to the questions and exercises, they are carefully designed to expand and challenge your thinking. You will find that some of the exercises are based on NLP (Neuro Linguistic Programming) interventions, given my background as a Master NLP Practitioner.

Is this book for you?

I am assuming you are reading this book for one of the following reasons, either because:
- You are considering a leadership role and want to prepare; or
- You have just been promoted to your first leadership role; or
- You are not progressing as quickly as you would like to; or
- You don't have time for theory but you do want some quick, practical solutions; or

- You are an HR professional looking for ways to help, develop and engage talented individuals.

Essentially, you are curious about how to create the maximum impact as quickly as possible, how to get the most from your team, and how to learn from the mistakes that others have already made.

Rules used in the book

- I use the title of manager and leader interchangeably, making the assumption that you are/will be responsible for leading a team of people.
- I mostly use the term 'he' when describing leaders purely for consistency, while recognising that there are many female leaders.
- The case studies have been created from actual coaching sessions. However, identities have been masked to ensure confidentiality, and sometimes two or more different issues have been incorporated into one story to illustrate a point.

I highly recommend that you record your thoughts and responses as you progress through the chapters, ideally writing in a personal journal. The suggested exercises broadly reflect some of those which I typically use with clients, although unlike working with a personal coach, they have not been tailored to an individual. When you consider the questions, give yourself space to think, and note your reflections, not only will you be enhancing your performance and success at work, but you will also begin to notice improvements in other areas of your life.

Enjoy the journey!

PART ONE
Preparing for Leadership

CHAPTER ONE

Setting the Foundations

"Leadership is the art of getting someone else to do something you want done, because he wants to do it."

Dwight D. Eisenhower

Leaders lead people and managers manage processes. This appears to be the most succinct and common distinction between the two titles, yet I find it difficult to define roles and responsibilities based upon titles, having coached managers who lead large teams, and some who have no-one reporting to them at all.

Whatever your current or anticipated title, I am making the assumption that you are about to have, or already have, a team of people reporting to you. Your first time managing and leading a team, whatever the size, can be one of the most difficult periods of adjustment in your career. Approaching leadership was recently described to me as preparing to "stand at the top of the pile and be shot at", an interesting perception!

When you are new to leadership, your world will change from being self-centric to putting others first. Getting to grips with your new role will be easier, and more productive, as you develop the skills required to be a strong leader of people, not just a manager of processes.

1. SOFT SKILLS FOR STRONG LEADERS

It is natural to assume that technical expertise, hard work, and enthusiasm will help you to progress up the career ladder. Yes, these are all important, but they do not make a great leader. You might be able to get tasks completed, but do you have the necessary skills to deliver results through others?

Leaders are required to inspire and motivate others, to get *"someone else to do something you want done, because he wants to do it"*. In order to get people *"to do something"*, it helps to recognise what drives their behaviour, and to understand what compels them to take action, without you having to constantly push and cajole. This is where soft skills come in.

When you have the necessary soft skills, you will be able to influence those around you, to do what needs to be done. They will be more engaged, and will want to go the extra mile for you. Your unique range of soft skills will set you apart from those who have similar technical expertise and experience. You will be able to progress your career faster, and deliver results more easily, with the full support of those around you.

Soft skills will help you adapt to the constant changes around you, enabling you to become more creative, productive and resilient, and so better able to handle everyday challenges. When you have direct reports, you must master a wide range of management skills; managing the business, managing your team, and managing yourself.

So what is the difference between hard and soft skills?

Hard skills

Hard skills are the technical competencies and expertise which are required for your profession or industry. For example, a Human Resources Manager will require specific knowledge of employment law, recruitment and pensions. Hard skills are the result of tangible and measurable knowledge, gained from training and qualifications in a chosen field. Hard skills enable you to do your job by completing certain tasks, producing results and delivering outcomes.

Soft skills

Soft skills are your character traits, your interpersonal and communication skills. These are the visible behaviours, attitudes, and personal attributes that you demonstrate when interacting with others. They are more about who you are, rather than what you know, and are determined by your personality, values, beliefs, culture and experience.

Although we usually consider the term 'soft skills' in relation to how we communicate with others, the quality, and effectiveness, of our soft skills is reflected in how well we understand and communicate with ourselves. As a leader, before you can positively influence the behaviour of others, it helps to be aware of what drives your own behaviour.

Soft skills are difficult to evaluate, often being perceived as intrinsic. However, they can be developed if you have a strong desire and motivation to do so. If you are determined to be a great leader, then you will want to develop your soft skills.

2. EMOTIONAL INTELLIGENCE

Soft skills are often used to describe and measure a person's Emotional Intelligence (EI). This term was thought to have been created in the 1990s by Peter Salovey and John Meyer. They described Emotional Intelligence as *"a set of four inter-related abilities that involves the ability to perceive, use, understand, and manage emotions"*. The roots of EI can be traced back to Robert Thorndike in 1937, who wrote about 'Social Intelligence', but it was Daniel Goleman who popularised the term with his book **Emotional Intelligence – Why It Can Matter More Than IQ in 1996**.

Goleman stated, *"If your emotional abilities aren't in hand, if you don't have self-awareness, if you are not able to manage your distressing emotions, if you can't have empathy and have effective relationships, then no matter how smart you are, you are not going to get very far."* To explore this topic further, a good starting point is to read **Leadership: The Power of Emotional Intelligence** by Daniel Goleman.

Emotional Intelligence is not about being soft and fluffy, it is about behaving and interacting with others in an effective way that helps get the job done with ease. Emotionally intelligent leaders have finely-tuned people skills, and they lead with energy and motivation. Their teams perform better, contributing to employee engagement, productivity, and loyalty. They also have better relationships with their peers, their boss, other stakeholders in the organisation and customers.

The five components of Emotional Intelligence

1. Self-awareness - being aware of your own internal mood, your preferences, resources, and intuitions. This includes recognising your emotions and their effect on your behaviour, being aware of your strengths and limits, having a strong sense of self-worth, self-confidence, and knowing your capabilities.

2. Self-regulation - includes:
- Self-control - keeping strong and potentially disruptive emotions and impulses under control.
- Trustworthiness - maintaining standards of honesty and integrity.
- Conscientiousness - taking responsibility for your personal productivity and performance.
- Adaptability - being flexible when dealing with change.
- Innovation - being comfortable with new ideas, approaches and handling new information with ease.

3. Motivation - understanding what drives you to achieve your goals, or to take action. It includes:
- Achievement drive - stretching to meet or exceed a standard of excellence.
- Commitment - being aligned with goals of your team or organisation.
- Initiative - being ready to act when opportunities appear.
- Optimism - being positive and persistent in striving towards goals.

4. Social Awareness - picking up on what is going on for those around you.
- Empathy - sensing other's feelings, and taking an active interest in their needs and concerns.
- Service orientation - anticipating, recognising, and meeting client's needs.
- Leveraging diversity - developing opportunities through a variety of people.
- Political awareness - noticing a group's emotional needs and relationships.

5. Relationship Management - motivating others, leading and developing them. It also includes collaborating, confronting and facilitating relationships, influencing and persuading, and creating group synergy in pursuit of collective goals.

Throughout the book we will be exploring many of the attributes, attitudes, and characteristics that are encompassed in emotional and social intelligence. These skills are essential as you transition through the different stages of your career, as well as being incredibly useful life skills.

Where are the gaps?

The first step to developing your soft skills, and to understand which areas need working upon, is to assess your perceived current level of skill. This is, of course, subjective, so you may want to ask some colleagues for their opinion. Remember though, that it is merely 'their opinion', and not necessarily fact, but do be open to the concept that there might be some truth in their perception.

Pause here and take out your journal. Follow the instructions in the next exercise to assess your soft skills, and then ask someone you trust to give you their view.

Record their comments in your journal to compare with your own, along with your thoughts as you reflect on the two sets of scores.

Exercise 1.1 - Soft Skills Assessment

Review the list of common leadership characteristics and attributes.
Assess how satisfied you are with your ability to demonstrate each characteristic or attribute.
Rate your assessment on a scale of 1 - 10 (10 = high).

Adaptable	Inclusive
Assertive	Influencer
Authentic	Intuitive
Collaborative	Initiative
Committed	Innovative
Communicator	Integrity
Compassionate	Listens
Confident	Manages Stress
Conscientious	Manages Time
Courageous	Open
Creative	Optimistic
Decisive	Passionate
Delegates	Patient
Determined	Persistent
Develops others	Positive
Driven	Problem Solver
Empathetic	Purposeful
Energetic	Rapport Builder
Flexible	Reliable
Honest	Resilient
Humble	Respects others

Respects self	Self-esteem
Self-accepting	Self-motivated
Self-belief	Sensitive
Self-confident	Sincere
Self-control	Socially aware
Self-disciplined	Takes responsibility

1. Now, jot down in your journal which attributes you are most proud of and why.
2. Next consider which characteristics or attributes **you** think you need to develop.
3. How is this different to the views of other people?
4. Take the **top five attributes/skills** that you would like to develop, and describe in your journal what the difference will be, once you have enhanced these skills.
5. Record the date of your first assessment, and make a note to review your assessment at the end of the book, or after you have worked on some of these areas.

3. AUTHENTIC LEADERSHIP

It has been well documented that successful leaders are those who demonstrate authenticity. As you embark on your new leadership role, it will be useful to explore what this term means to you, and how you can develop your own authenticity.

To be 'authentic' is to be real, genuine, or original. To be an authentic leader is to be true to yourself, true to your values and beliefs, and this means that your leadership style will be unique to you. If you try to be someone you are not by putting on a facade, those around you will notice, and your leadership journey will be a more difficult and stressful one.

Why is it important to be authentic?

When you are authentic, those around you will want to follow you, and will be more prepared to go the extra mile for - and with - you. They will see you leading with purpose and integrity, aware that you follow through on your actions. They will know that you are looking out for them, and will trust and respect you. As you demonstrate honesty and transparency in your relationships, the effects will ripple out far beyond your immediate team. Your colleagues, clients, and your boss will look to you for guidance, and will value what you have to offer. Leading with authenticity helps to nurture your self-respect and self-worth, and this will enable you to maximise your impact in every aspect of your role.

Leading with authenticity comes naturally when you understand your purpose and have clarity in the direction you are taking. It is easier when your actions are underpinned by your values, and when you put your team members first. Being an authentic leader should not take effort when you have the courage to be who you really are.

As you consider your first leadership role, whether you are to be a supervisor, manager or team leader, this is the time to start raising your self-awareness of who you are, and how you operate as a person. Let us take some time to explore what is important to you, and what you believe in, so that you can ensure you develop a leadership style that is consistent with your character and personality.

4. LEADERSHIP VALUES

Your core values are those aspects important to you in any context of your life – we talk about these later in the book – whereas leadership values are important to you in your leadership role. Before you step up as a leader, consider what is important to you about the role of a leader, and reflect upon whether your current actions demonstrate those values. If you want to be an authentic leader, start by being seen as a person who is true to both their core and leadership values.

Typical leadership values might include courage, integrity, leading by example, innovation, and helping others to grow. Although these are 'typical' and tend to underpin the behaviour of many strong leaders, you will have your own unique list of values.

It is helpful to understand what **your** leadership values are, what they really mean to you, and **why** they are important to you, so that you can ensure your actions are in alignment with them. Being aware of these values will also help you to understand why certain situations annoy, irritate or frustrate you.

Imagine that one of your top leadership values is honesty. If you find out that one of your team has been over-claiming on expenses, how do you react? I assume that you will deal with the situation sharply and effectively, communicating that such behaviour is totally unacceptable. However, if honesty is not one of your top values, then you will still deal with the situation, but not with such a high priority.

Conflicting values

You will know when your values are being compromised because something will not feel right. You may feel anxious, guilty or fearful, or you may feel deflated and de-motivated, but confused as to the reason why.

It is not uncommon to experience such niggles, but we often ignore them, hoping they will go away. If these feelings are left unchecked, they will continue to crop up, developing into anxiety or stress. This could then manifest into poor sleep patterns, ulcers and other physical ailments. So what can you do about conflicting values?

When you notice an inner unease, pay attention to the feeling, and explore what is causing it. What is underlying that feeling? What have you been thinking about to cause it? If you can identify it, consider what, if any, action you need to take, or whether you need to change your thinking or behaviour. When you are not being authentic, it is as if your 'real self' is being hidden away. It is not just your body and your state of mind that will suffer - it will also impact on those around you. If you are not being honest with your team - maybe you are holding back certain information - then they will pick up on this, and will start to worry about what you are not telling them, jumping to their own conclusions.

If you have ever experienced a role, or worked for a company, where one of your top values has not been fulfilled, then when looking for your next role, it will be very important that this value is present. This was the situation with Alison in the case study below.

Alison

Alison came for coaching initially because she was feeling stuck and frustrated in her current role. She didn't feel as though she was being challenged or stretched enough and knew that promotion was unlikely due to the flat organisational structure where she worked. She was ready for more responsibility and wanted to feel that she was contributing to the direction of a company. She was keen to explore and develop the skills she needed to progress.

We started to dig a little deeper, to uncover what was causing Alison to feel stuck and frustrated. In addition to the lack of career opportunities, she shared with me that new procedures had been introduced which didn't sit comfortably with her. Headcount had been cut to reduce overheads, her workload had been increased, and customer care was suffering.

I took Alison through an exercise to understand her work values. Included in her top five work values were progression, creativity, and making a difference. None of these values were being met in her current role, so it was no wonder Alison was feeling frustrated and de-motivated.

As Alison was aspiring to apply for roles with more responsibility, and in particular she wanted to lead a team, we explored her leadership values. We followed a similar exercise to the one below.

Exercise 1.2 - Your Unique Set of Leadership Values

Start to develop your own authenticity by determining what your leadership values are. To help you with the process, think about bosses you have worked for in the past, or other leaders that you know now. Record your responses in your journal.

- What attributes or characteristics did they demonstrate, that you value and respect?
- What made them a good leader in your eyes?
- What could they have done better or done more of?

Bearing this in mind, now consider:
1. What is important to **you** about being a leader, and how you want to lead **your** team?
2. What is important to you about how you are treated, and

how you treat other people?
3. When you are feeling totally motivated, what is the emotion behind this, and what activity are you involved in at the time?

Keep asking yourself these three questions until you have up to 20 responses, then hone down each response or phrase, to one or two word answers.

Examples of values are: *equality, integrity, responsibility, accuracy, respect, diversity, improvement, fun, credibility, honesty, innovativeness, teamwork, excellence, accountability, empowerment, efficiency, dignity, collaboration, empathy, achievement, courage, wisdom, independence, challenge, influence, learning, growth, compassion, generosity, patience, persistence, optimism, flexibility, recognition, creativity.*

Now pick out your top ten values, and write each one down on a small piece of paper. Underneath the value heading, e.g. 'Integrity', write a paragraph to describe what this means to you. Consider what behaviours demonstrate that you have integrity.

On the reverse side, write a paragraph to explain WHY this value is important to you. This will help to clarify **what** each word means to you, and **why** it is important.

The next step is to prioritise your list. Take your first value, put it down on the table, and then place the next value either above or below it, depending on whether it is more or less important. Repeat the exercise until you have all of your values in priority order, with the most important at the top. Record or place your top ten values in your journal.

Alison

By uncovering Alison's leadership values, she was able to articulate what was important to her about the kind of role she was looking for, and the kind of leader she wanted to be. Included in Alison's top ten leadership values were collaboration, transparency, and creativity.

By defining these, we could explore what they meant to Alison, and what kind of role would enable her to live these values on a daily basis.

Do you 'walk the talk'?

You should now have your prioritised list of values, aware what each means, plus why it is important to you. Now consider whether your behaviour and actions as a leader, and as an individual, are in alignment.

If 'courage' is in your top ten, what are you currently doing to demonstrate courage? Do you stick your neck out when you do not agree with something? Are you willing to make a tough decision when it might not be popular? If one of your values is to 'lead by example', what are you doing that demonstrates this? Are you prepared to roll your sleeves up, and do the tasks that you might ask your team to do? Are you a good role model? How do you know?

When you have your list of leadership values, you can monitor your own behaviour, and notice the impact that it is having on those around you. When you demonstrate clearly that you lead with purpose, how does your team react? Even if you are not yet in a leadership role, you can start behaving like a leader now.

Communicating values

Be prepared to communicate your top leadership values to your new team and find out what is important to them too. This way you can start to create a culture of transparency, manage expectations, and share what is important to each of you. They will be more motivated to work effectively as a team because they feel included, acknowledged, and listened to.

When you decide to consciously develop your authenticity, you will become more aware of your behaviour, the behaviour of others, and how you are reacting to situations and people around you.

Paying attention to feelings

How will you know when you are being truly authentic? Well, you have already started the process by defining your leadership values, exploring what is important to you, and how you can demonstrate this in your day-to-day behaviour. Because so many of our behaviours and actions are unconscious, it is important to check in regularly with how you are feeling about different situations and decisions, to gauge whether that feeling or reaction feels 'right', and more importantly whether it feels authentic and in alignment with your values.

Exercise 1.3 - Living your Values

If you are not sure whether some of your actions are truly authentic, try this exercise.

1. Consider an event/situation that you have experienced recently i.e.
- Giving constructive feedback.
- Making a difficult decision.
- Attending a board meeting.
- Conducting a team meeting.
- A client visit.
- Attending a networking event.
2. Now refer to your top five leadership values.
3. Reflect on the chosen event/situation and ask yourself, "In what way did I conduct myself that demonstrated my top leadership values?"
4. If you were not behaving in a way that reflects your values, consider what you will do differently next time.
5. Record your thoughts in your journal.

When you are being authentic, you will notice a positive reaction from those around you. You are a role model to your team, whether you intend to be or not. The more genuine and transparent you are, the more they will be too. When you take responsibility for your actions, you will notice how your authenticity impacts on team performance and productivity, and you will notice how problems and difficult situations get easier.

Alison

Alison was eventually successful in finding a new role that included leading a small team. She returned for some more coaching sessions four months into the new position. Our initial sessions had helped Alison to get clarity on the kind of organisation and the type of role she wanted to pursue. Alison had given a lot of thought to her leadership values, and once in the new organisation she shared these with her team, checking that she also understood what was important to them. This process fitted well to demonstrate Alison's values of transparency and collaboration.

When Alison returned to coaching, she was sensing some frustration and de-motivation. Because we had talked previously about paying attention to internal conflicts, Alison realised that it was because she was so overwhelmed with tasks to do, there was little time to spare for being creative – this was one of Alison's top five values.

We set about improving Alison's time management and self-imposed expectations (we talk about these topics later on). Once Alison felt more confident to delegate some of her tasks, and developed a more rational approach to her need for perfection, she was able to allocate a regular space in her diary for reflection and creativity.

Alison continues to refer to her values on a regular basis by making time for self reflection. She now solicits feedback from her boss and peers to ensure that her behaviour is in alignment with her leadership values, and with the help of a highly motivated and engaged team she is delivering great results for the company.

5. A LEADING PERSONALITY

In preparation for your first leadership role, it is useful to consider whether you have a natural leadership personality style. Many great leaders tend to be more extroverted, they are goal focused, visionary and creative. They have a good balance between valuing rationale and seeking harmony, they are organised, and motivated by seeing projects through to completion.

Do you find it easy to step back and look at the bigger picture, without getting bogged down in the detail? When you make your decisions, do you carefully analyse the information available, or do you rely on gut instinct? Are you a 'people person', or are you more introverted, preferring to immerse yourself in books and research?

There will be aspects of your new role which will challenge you. Perhaps you are not a natural strategic thinker, quick at making decisions or comfortable giving feedback. It could be that these situations are stretching because you have never experienced them before, or it could be that the skills required are not your natural preference.

Personality profiling tools

There are many personality profiling tools available to raise your self-awareness of your existing leadership style. By completing a short questionnaire, you can uncover your natural style, identifying your strengths, plus highlighting those areas which may need more work. This can act as a starting point to help you enhance skills such as communication, decision-making, problem-solving, and influencing others. It will also help you to recognise patterns of behaviour that work well for you, and understand those that hold you back.

One of the tools I use is TDI 'Type Dynamic Indicator', a comprehensive approach to measuring Psychological Type, based on the work of Carl Jung. It is considered to be an updated alternative to Myers Briggs (MBTI). TDI is a proven framework for raising self-awareness, and enables the individual to make more conscious choices about the way they approach their work and their lives.

What is Type theory?

TDI is based on 'Type' theory. It is built on the concept of opposites, and the nature of preference. The report assesses style and preferences, not ability or competence. Just as we can choose between using our left or right hand, the theory suggests that we can choose between using opposite sides of our character. If it feels more natural to use your right hand, you will use your left hand less, and yet you can still use both if necessary.

Jung proposes that this applies to personality, and our choices involve the following four pairs of opposite personality styles:

Extraversion (E) and Introversion (I) - From where do you get your energy?
- Do you thrive when there is a lot going on, or do you prefer a quieter environment?
- Do you prefer discussion and interaction with others, or time to reflect?
- Do you seek out the buzz of activity, or do you enjoy solitude and silence?

Sensing (S) and iNtuition (N) - How do you perceive the world?
- Do you focus on the facts and the detail, or upon the big picture?
- Are you practical and down-to-earth, or do you prefer new ideas and the future?
- Are you happy to deal with routines, or do you prefer novelty?

Thinking (T) and Feeling (F) – How do you make your decisions?
- Do you need rationale and logical analysis, or do you focus on values, relationships and feelings?
- Do you base decisions on objectivity, or subjectivity?
- Do you need to know the logic, or do you prefer to understand the value?

Judging (J) and Perceiving (P) – How do you manage the world around you?
- Do you like to plan, or to play it by ear?
- Are you motivated by reaching the end goal, or by starting a new project?
- Are you frustrated when interrupted, or do you welcome the distraction?

When you put the four preferred letters together, you arrive at your personality type code, which can be any one of sixteen combinations. For example, INTJ indicates that you prefer Introversion, Intuition, Thinking and Judging. Remember, this indicates preferences only, someone with a reported type INTJ also uses the extraversion, sensing, feeling and perception sides of their personality, but to a lesser degree.

It is possible for your profile to change as you develop your ideas about what is most important and rewarding to you, and as you develop and adapt your styles and behaviours.

Uncovering your personality style is not only useful to understand how you work best (or what is stopping you from achieving your best), it can also help you to understand how your colleagues are working, and respect each other's differences.

There are many psychometric personality profiling tools available, including popular tools such as MBTI, DISC, TDI and Insights, all of which are incredibly useful in helping to raise your self-awareness. If you are interested, there is a wealth of information about these tools on the internet.

Thinking like a leader

Even if you are not a leader or manager yet, assuming you have completed the exercises to date, you will be starting to think like a leader. You will be more aware of the soft skills that require your attention. You have defined your leadership values and will be starting to recognise your natural personality style, and how this can contribute to your success.

Summary

1. Soft skills are more about who you are, rather than what you know.
2. Emotionally intelligent leaders have finely-tuned people skills - they lead with energy and motivation.
3. Review **Exercise 1.1 - Soft Skills Assessment** regularly, and request feedback from those around you.
4. To be an authentic leader is to be true to yourself, true to your values and beliefs, which means that your leadership style is going to be unique to you.
5. Refer to your leadership values periodically so that you can reflect upon, and monitor, your own behaviour, noticing the impact that it is having on those around you.
6. Pay attention to feelings of unease, it could be that your values are being compromised.
7. Uncover your preferred personality style to understand your natural strengths, and those areas which need developing to be a strong leader.

CHAPTER TWO

Managing your Mindset

"It's not who you are that holds you back, it's who you think you're not."

Attributed to Hanoch McCarty

As you approach a new leadership role, you will probably experience a wide range of emotions. You may be looking forward to the challenge ahead with quiet confidence, or you may be apprehensive, quietly suppressing a lack of self-belief.

Despite putting on a brave face and portraying an air of confidence to the outside world, I meet many new (and older, experienced) leaders, who deep down, are wondering, *"Can I really do this?"*, *"Will they find me out?"* Whether you are in the first three months of your new post, or at some later stage in your career, it is not unusual to experience self-doubt.

Having uncovered your leadership values in Chapter One, and knowing what it takes to be an authentic leader, can you stay grounded in your true identity? Will you be able to hold on to your values, adopt the most empowering thoughts and beliefs, and maintain a healthy level of self-esteem? Your ability to exude confidence will be particularly important when you have tough decisions to make, and when you are being closely judged by those around you.

1. SELF-ESTEEM AND CONFIDENCE

Maintaining a healthy self-esteem is essential when you are in a leadership role, it will have a major bearing upon how you act and react, and therefore, the results you can achieve. Self-esteem is often confused with confidence, and although the two are inter-linked, there is a subtle difference.

What is the difference?

Self-esteem is a measure of how you see and feel about yourself, on the inside. Do you see yourself as intelligent and courageous? Or, do you secretly see yourself as a fraud? Your own perceptions and thoughts will either have a negative, or a positive effect on how you feel, and therefore, how you behave. Self-confidence is the measure of how much trust and faith you have in yourself and your abilities, and how you project yourself to the outside world.

I meet many leaders who act confidently, but confess to not feeling it inside. There is a saying *"fake it 'till you make it"*, which simply means pretending you are confident, until it becomes a habit, and starts to feel genuine. I, however, prefer to tackle confidence issues from the inside, working on developing self-esteem, and controlling the inner dialogue. If you can achieve this, you will have more trust and faith in yourself, and therefore your actions will come across as more confident and authentic.

Self-esteem

The word 'Esteem' comes from the Latin *Aestimare* 'to put a value on' and it shares the same root as the verb 'to estimate'. To hold someone 'in esteem', means that you value and respect them. Self-esteem (or self-worth) is quite literally, the estimated value you place on yourself.

Self-esteem is influenced by what you believe to be true about yourself. It grows from respecting and accepting yourself, and by taking responsibility for your actions.

It is also affected by how others treat you, and how you feel about yourself when you are with them. Self-esteem will affect how you interact with others, how you live your life, at home, and at work.

Your level of self-esteem will fluctuate, particularly as you are placed in different situations, and compare yourself to those around you. Have you noticed that, in certain environments, or with certain people, you are confident and happy to be the centre of attention?

At other times though, you feel reserved, and reluctant to share your ideas?

Your natural level of self-esteem will have been developed and influenced by your formative experiences and relationships. The good news is that you can enhance it, once you learn how to respect and accept yourself, taking responsibility for where you are, and who you are, right now.

Mark

Operations Manager Mark requested a coaching programme to help address some personal issues that were affecting his performance at work. As we worked together, Mark shared that he was feeling de-motivated, having recently been overlooked for promotion. He had worked for the organisation for over 6 years, had a wealth of knowledge, and was often invited to meetings normally reserved for executive board members.

Mark was frustrated that he had to report to someone who was less experienced than himself, but wasn't sure what to do next. He was performing the role of a senior leader, he was included in top level discussions, but he was not being rewarded financially, nor was he receiving the recognition he felt he deserved.

Although on a conscious level, Mark knew that he was good at what he did, unconsciously he didn't believe he was good enough. Otherwise, he reasoned that by now, he would have been acknowledged by his boss for his valuable contribution, and promoted. Mark was reluctant to make a fuss in case it back-fired on him, and made him look unprofessional. This was now affecting his confidence, and he was seriously considering looking for another job.

People with a high self-esteem have a strong sense of 'self'; they like and respect themselves, they can recognise and manage their internal feelings, and they have a clear sense of purpose. How often do you stop to value and appreciate the kind of person you are?

This is an exercise that I took Mark through, helping him to acknowledge and appreciate the qualities he was most proud of.

Exercise 2.1 - Blow your own Trumpet

Take your journal and write out the top ten attributes, or qualities, that you recognise and appreciate about yourself. These might include: *my sense of humour, my physique, my smile, I'm a good listener, I get on with most people, I'm hardworking, I always go the extra mile, I'm passionate about what I do, I get results, I'm focused, I'm trustworthy.*
What are **your** top ten?

1. _____
2. _____
3. _____
4. _____
5. _____
6. _____
7. _____
8. _____
9. _____
10. _____

Read out each line to yourself, out loud if possible, and say to yourself: "I respect myself because I am "X" (i.e. passionate about what I do)".

> Now add the word 'because' and then continue the sentence with evidence to back up this fact, reminding yourself of what it is you do to demonstrate this.
>
> Continue with each attribute, and expand on each one as you read them out loud, or quietly to yourself. Note down what your thoughts are as you read these out. What are you noticing?

Some people find this exercise quite difficult, as they are more used to criticising what they do, or what they look like, and prefer to focus on what they do not like about themselves.

When you start to appreciate, respect, and value who you are, and what you do to help others, your self-esteem will start to expand. This is not bragging, it is simply recognising your strengths, and loving who you are.

Self-acceptance

We are constantly judging and evaluating ourselves, usually in comparison to others. Your opinion of yourself will fluctuate from day-to-day, even hour by hour, affected by events and encounters with other people. Some people may be smarter, more attractive, or more articulate than you. Others might have achieved more than you have, but if you continue to compare yourself with them, this will erode your self-esteem, and your behaviour will become less confident. Although you cannot fundamentally change yourself, you can alter the way you perceive yourself, and you can choose how you make sense of those perceptions.

Learning to respect and accept yourself for who you are, recognising and acknowledging your weaknesses as well as your strengths, is the foundation of self-regard. When you have a high self-regard, it makes it easier for you to have a high regard for others, accepting them for who they are and respecting their uniqueness. This is a key leadership quality.

Traits of high self-esteem

People with high self-esteem usually...
- Have a quiet confidence.
- Do not fish for compliments, but they do accept them.
- May be quite humble.
- Appreciate and are often interested in other people and their achievements.
- Are less concerned about receiving external recognition.
- Are relaxed, upright, calm, measured in movement, decisive and without hesitation.

These people do not need to prove themselves, and do not look for outside approval.
This means that they generally DO NOT...
- Boast
- Put others down
- Show off
- Name-drop
- Hog the conversation

Even people who are outwardly competent and confident, secretly doubt themselves and their capabilities. They will often stand up for others, but not for themselves. When you have a healthy self-esteem and self-respect, you will be ready to stand up for yourself too.

Achievements

Now that you recognise and appreciate your wealth of skills and strengths, let us look at your achievements. What have you achieved in the last two years? An achievement can be anything that you are proud of, for example, big work projects, qualifications, moving house, securing a sought-after role, designing your garden. We all interpret the word 'achievement' differently, what does it means to you?

How often do you spend time setting goals, work hard to achieve them, and then move on to the next one, without stopping to notice your successes? Isn't it time to give yourself a big pat on the back? This is a great habit to get into on a daily, weekly, or monthly basis.

Make time to reflect

Imagine spending just ten minutes at the end of the day, sitting back and reflecting on what you have achieved. How would this make you feel? There will be days when it seems as if you have been running from one meeting to the next, not achieving much, but when you take the time to stop and think, you will come up with a list of achievements. When you do this on a daily basis, it means you are focusing on positive aspects of the day, rather than noticing what you have not done. Which makes you feel better? As you reflect on your achievements, notice what skills and resources you used to do this. What skills do you use on a daily basis, that come naturally to you? Do you have good interpersonal skills, mental skills, or are you better at using your hands? You can add these to your previous list of what you appreciate about yourself.

Maintaining a healthy self-esteem is of paramount importance when you are in a leadership role. Revisit these exercises when you find yourself in a period of self-doubt, and remind yourself how unique and talented you really are.

You can read more about self esteem in *Six Pillars of Self-Esteem by Nathaniel Branden*.

Increasing self-confidence

Your self-confidence levels will rise as your self-esteem grows. Here are some tips to increase your self-confidence.

Top Tips - Increase your Self-Confidence

- Ensure you complete **Exercise 2.1 - Blow your own Trumpet**.
- Set yourself stretching, yet achievable goals.
- Stop and acknowledge your achievements.
- Step out of your comfort zone, at least twice a day.
- Let go of trying to be perfect, and feeling you have to do everything yourself.
- Recognise where you shine, and put yourself in those situations as often as possible.
- Read the next section on Limiting Beliefs, and create some new empowering beliefs to increase your confidence.

Mark

Coaching helped Mark to understand what was stopping him from sharing his frustration with his line manager, and the HR department. Although on a conscious level, he knew that he was doing a good job, he didn't really believe he was good enough, otherwise in his eyes, he would have been promoted.

Once Mark began to share and acknowledge his skills and the contribution he had made over the past six years, his self-esteem soared, and his confidence grew, enabling him to have an honest conversation with his line manager and CEO. By valuing himself and being more assertive, he was able to put forward a solid case for promotion, which was successful.

When you value, accept and respect yourself, others will value, accept and respect you too.

2. MANAGING YOUR MINDSET

Have you noticed that you are thinking all the time? Your mind never seems to switch off. You are either thinking about situations which happened in the past, or considering what you are about to do next. You will be judging other people and situations, judging yourself based on how you see yourself and how you think others are judging you.

Everything you do, all of your actions, and all of your behaviours, are driven by your thoughts, whether conscious or unconscious. Your thoughts are the result of how you perceive the world around you, your values and beliefs, your experience, your knowledge and your culture.

Controlling your thoughts

These thoughts can be empowering or limiting, and sometimes downright destructive. Your thoughts kick in as soon as you wake up, and do not stop until you finally drift off in the evening. Sometimes they prevent you from going to sleep, they may wake you in the night, and even occupy your dreams.

If you stop and pay attention to how you are feeling, and then notice carefully what you are thinking about, you can control your thoughts. Your internal chatter has a substantial impact on how you feel, and how you behave, which in turn, determines the results you can achieve.

Your inner critic

As you were completing the previous exercises, did you hear that little voice saying *"Yes, but…"* reminding you of the attributes you do not like about yourself, or recalling the times you did not achieve something you set out to do?

This inner dialogue, the part of you which is 'keeping your feet on the ground' exists for a reason. Consider what it could be doing for you, in a positive way? Although you may want to get rid of it, until you accept and acknowledge it's purpose, you will find it difficult to let it go.

How can you suppress that often negative and critical voice? A powerful strategy is to choose a funny or ridiculous sounding voice, maybe your favourite comedian or cartoon character, one that really makes you laugh. Practise saying the negative words/phrase (i.e. *"Yes, but I will probably mess it up…"*) with the funny voice, and notice how it makes you smile. It is more difficult to take the silly voice seriously, isn't it?

Christine

Christine had recently been promoted to the role of IT Director, and had been offered a coaching programme to support her through the transition. In one of our early meetings, Christine shared that she had an important presentation to make to a room full of senior directors.

Although she was used to making presentations, and had attended a presentation skills workshop, she was still feeling very anxious about standing up in front of a crowded room, which she knew would impact on her delivery. She knew her subject well, and had prepared for the anticipated questions, but wasn't sure what more she could do to generate the confidence she needed.

When I asked Christine to imagine that she was about to step onto the stage, and then to notice how she was feeling and what was going through her mind, Christine realised that her head was full of chatter. She was worrying whether she was wearing the right suit, what would the audience think of her if she stumbled on her words, what would happen if she couldn't answer the questions asked? She was starting to doubt whether she could deliver the presentation with the impact she knew it required.

Every passing thought about the forthcoming presentation was making Christine feel very anxious; her heart was pounding and her palms became clammy. It was as if she was looking at herself from the outside, judging herself harshly, and believing that her audience would be.

3. LIMITING BELIEFS

Christine's fears were based on her beliefs about herself, and about how others would judge her. We all have them, so where do these beliefs come from?

Similar to our values, our beliefs develop as we grow up. They come from our parents, family, teachers, friends, and other people who were, and often still are, significant in our lives. For example, if your parents held the belief that life was hard, then this is also likely to be your belief. If you were told at school that you would not amount to much, you may still be trying to prove yourself, believing deep down that you do not deserve to be successful – there are many adults who are still trying to prove themselves to their parents.

A belief is simply your opinion, it is not an absolute fact.
- *"I believe the sun will rise tomorrow"*, is not a belief, it is a fact.
- *"I believe I'm going to mess up this presentation"*, is not a fact, it is your opinion.

Perhaps this limiting belief is based on evidence from a previous presentation which did not go too well, but that evidence may also be based on an event that happened years ago, and is no longer relevant.

The good news is that you can change your beliefs, if you choose to. Your old beliefs might be negative and limiting, but they also might be protecting you in some way, and it is useful to find out what their positive intention is. Once you understand the positive intention, i.e. how that belief is benefiting you, you can also decide whether this belief is still relevant, and whether it is empowering or limiting you. And of course you can decide whether you are willing, and ready, to change it.

Try this exercise to change limiting beliefs that may be stopping you from progressing.

Exercise 2.2 - Changing your Beliefs

Make a short list in your journal, of beliefs you have about a key capability or skill that you lack, or feel is holding you back in some way. Maybe you believe that you are not good at managing meetings or presenting to a large audience? What are you assuming to be true that is stopping you from applying for a more senior role?
For example:
1. I find it difficult to make decisions quickly
2. I don't handle conflict very well
3. I'm not good at giving presentations
4. I freeze when I'm put on the spot

Now consider for each belief
- Is this belief helping or hindering you?
- What are the benefits of holding on to this belief?
- Is this absolute fact, or is it your opinion?
- Where did this belief come from? Were you told this at an early age, or is it a belief you have adopted from someone else?
- Do you have any hard evidence for this belief? Is it still valid today?

When you have a limiting belief about your ability, and you remind yourself about this belief, your unconscious mind will take notice and produce the behaviour to back up your belief. If you keep telling yourself that you're not very creative, your unconscious mind will think, *"OK, let's not bother trying, because we can't do this anyway!"*

If your list contains beliefs and opinions that are limiting, you **can** choose to change them - if you want to - and choose some more empowering beliefs. If you were to change the limiting examples above to: *"I am creative"*, or *"I am an articulate presenter"*, then you will start to find the evidence to back up these new positive beliefs.

Ensure your new beliefs are personal to you, framed in the positive tense, short and punchy.
What are **your** new beliefs? Record your thoughts in your journal.

As we have already discussed, your thoughts and beliefs have a big impact on how you are feeling, which in turn impacts on your behaviour, and therefore it is essential that you recognise when you are feeling 'out of sorts'. When you feel this, examine carefully what you are thinking about. If you are feeling anxious, I can guarantee that you are not thinking positive, or empowering thoughts!

Christine

Christine realised that her anxiety about the presentation flared up as soon as she started to worry about how she would come across. Her mind chatter was full of limiting beliefs and assumptions, such as:
- *I'll be so nervous that I know I'll stumble over my words.*
- *They will think I'm boring.*
- *What if they ask me questions I can't answer?*

She realised that these thoughts were not helping her to be the relaxed, yet professional, presenter that she wanted to be. Christine was ready to let go of her limiting beliefs, and I worked with her to

change them to more empowering ones. She created a mental strategy so that as she approached the stage, she would be repeating to herself:
- *I am speaking loudly and clearly so they can hear me.*
- *They have come to listen to me because they are interested in what I have to say.*
- *I am fully prepared.*

Thinking these new thoughts gave Christine a sense of calm and inner confidence, and freed her mind to focus on the content of the presentation. Glowing feedback following the presentation proved that Christine's new beliefs helped her to come across as the intelligent and confident leader she really is.

If you want to change how you feel, you must change what you are thinking about.

Assumptions & mind-reading

We make many assumptions and judgements about the world around us, about people, situations and how we fit in. Our assumptions and perceptions are unique to each of us, based on our background, culture, experiences, values, beliefs and personality type. We all have our own 'model of the world', based on our perspectives, and how we take in the information presented to us.

Your beliefs about the world and those around you, are based on unconscious assumptions. I am asking you to challenge these assumptions, if they are holding you back from achieving what you want.

The key question to ask yourself is: "What am I assuming to be true about this situation?" This will uncover your beliefs, which you can then scrutinise, and consider whether they are actually fact or an out-dated opinion.

For example, imagine you have been summoned to a meeting with your new boss and you are not sure why. Your natural reaction may be to feel anxious, and as you start to ponder what the reason might be, this means that you have already started mind-reading. What thoughts will be running through your mind to cause this anxiety? As you consider these thoughts, what are you *assuming* to be true?

Possible assumptions could be:
- The meeting is to discuss your performance so far.
- There is a problem with one of your team members.
- The client you saw on Friday was not happy with your presentation.

More often than not you will be expecting the worse.

What other reasons, more positive reasons, might there be?
- Your boss wants to ask your opinion on a project.
- He wants to share some good news with you.
- He has an update on your last meeting.

Whatever the reason, you do not know until you walk in the door, until you have the meeting, you are simply mind-reading. There is a reason for assuming the worst, and that is so that you are prepared for whatever you think may be about to happen. This is fine as long as it is not having a negative impact on your behaviour.

Christine

Christine had been mind-reading that the senior leaders would think she was boring, but once she was able to let go of these assumptions and find more useful 'mind-reads', i.e. 'They are attending the presentation because they are interested in what I have to say', she could let go of her anxiety.

Now that you are aware of mind-reading habits, and how you may already be imagining how a situation will unravel, you will be aware of the inner feeling this generates. If you notice you have a negative feeling, whether it is anxiety, guilt, or fear of making a decision, be curious about the thoughts you are focusing on. This self-awareness allows you to explore more positive assumptions, and will free you up to take the necessary action with confidence.

4. SETTING YOUR INTENTIONS

Have you noticed that you get what you focus on? When you go into a meeting that you expect to be long and boring, funnily enough it probably will end up being long and boring. If you are expecting an interview to be difficult, then it probably will be. We get what we expect to get, and we get what we focus our attention on, so wouldn't it be a good idea to change what we are expecting to get?

If you are going to learn how to manage your mindset effectively, you must set your intention by deciding what you want, believe that it is possible and focus your attention on achieving it.

Exercise 2.3 - Setting your Intentions

Think about a situation or event coming up, maybe a presentation, an interview or something that you would rather put off. If you are not looking forward to it, your focus will be on the expectation of an unpleasant / difficult / 'X' (you fill in the blanks) presentation or interview.

Whatever you think will happen in the meeting, it probably will. Maybe you are expecting to be asked difficult questions, or that you will 'mess up' in some way. Some of these thoughts may be based on what has happened in the past, and so you could have good reason to be thinking like this. But these thoughts are not helping you to perform at your best. Your internal chatter will create a certain negative feeling, maybe one of anxiety, frustration, or a fear of some kind. Your behaviour will reflect how you are feeling, therefore impact on the end result.

How would you like the event to happen instead?
Do you want...
- Your presentation to be well received?
- To come across as confident and articulate?
- Remain calm and in control?

Jot down what your ideal outcome or intention is. Ensure that you frame this in positive terms, and in the present tense. Imagine feeling that you have already achieved what you set out to achieve.

For example:
I am presenting calmly and with confidence.
My presentation is being well received.

Whatever your desired outcome, build up the picture in your mind of what you want to happen, how you are behaving, and how it feels to have achieved the outcome.
Now decide what empowering beliefs will help you to achieve this outcome, and jot these down.

Once you are in the actual situation, notice how it plays out as you imagined it would.

To expand on this exercise, skip forward to Chapter Eight, **Exercise 8.1 - Creating the Future.**

Frame your intentions positively

When you are focusing on ideal outcomes and setting your intention, the key is to frame your thoughts positively. If I asked you **not** to think of a pink cat sat on a yellow car, your mind will initially create an image of the pink cat on the yellow car, before acknowledging the command **not** to think about it. In fact, your unconscious mind does not process the words 'not/don't/none'. It is interesting that even when I am typing a sentence including such words, I seem to type the sentence without them, and then have to backtrack to correct it.

A good way to adopt a positive mindset, is to focus on your achievements as you did earlier, whether they are large or small. At the end of each day/week, or even after a tough meeting, rather than focusing on what went wrong (which seems to be a natural instinct), make a list of went well, and specifically what you did to contribute. You will feel much more upbeat.

Learning from mistakes

No matter how much you plan, and despite setting your positive intention, there are some things that are outside of your control and which will go wrong. If you have a tendency to dwell on this, as we are all capable of doing at times, then it can throw up all sorts of negative feelings – frustration, anger, anxiety – and cause a serious dent to your confidence.

It is useful to notice what has gone wrong, as long as you use these thoughts wisely. Remember that there is no such thing as failure, it is feedback. This means that when you do not get the result you desire, acknowledge what you tried to do to get that result, and notice what circumstances contributed to that outcome.

An authentic leader knows that it is okay to admit to mistakes, as long as they learn from them, and apply that learning to the next situation. Keep monitoring your results, notice what works and do more of it. Recognise what has not worked, and be flexible enough to make the necessary changes.

Summary

1. Self-esteem is built on self-respect, self-acceptance and self-responsibility.
2. People with a high self-esteem have a strong sense of self; they like themselves, they can recognise and manage their internal state and they have a clear sense of purpose.
3. When you experience times of self-doubt, refer back to **Exercise 2.1 – Blow your own Trumpet!**

4. Your internal chatter has a substantial impact on how you feel, and how you behave, which in turn, determines the results you can achieve.
5. Challenge the negative beliefs and assumptions that may be holding you back.
6. You get what you expect to get, and what you focus your attention on. So make sure that you focus on what you **do** want, not what you **do not** want.
7. Take responsibility for your own behaviour, and be willing to hold your hands up when you get it wrong.
8. Spend ten minutes at the end of the day reflecting on what has gone well, and what you have achieved.

CHAPTER THREE

Developing your Personal Brand

"When you are content to be simply yourself and don't compare or compete, everyone will respect you."

Lao Tzu

Do you remember your first boss? Did he inspire, motivate, or intimidate you? Was he larger than life, or did he blend into the background? Was he immaculately turned out, or non-descript in appearance? Did he interact well with staff, or stay hidden away in his ivory tower? Did he micromanage you, or encourage you to make your own decisions, learning from your own mistakes along the way? Did he even know your name?

I remember my first boss; he was strict, he knew everything that was going on, and he was always impeccably dressed. He was known for having very high standards, and was tough on those who failed to meet them. But he was fair, he listened, he asked constructive questions, and we all knew where we stood with him. When he walked into a room, people snapped to attention; when he asked for something to be done, it would always get done; when he himself agreed to take action, he always followed through. I do not recall particularly liking him, but I certainly respected and trusted him. He had a presence, I wanted to be on the right side of him, and I was willing to go the extra mile to be acknowledged and appreciated by him.

1. YOUR PERSONAL BRAND

Your personal brand is what you are known for - your reputation. It is what you stand for, and what makes you stand out. Your brand is unique and it is personal to you.

A personal brand is also about presence - how others unconsciously perceive you, the impact that you have on them. People will be influenced by what they see, what they hear, or how they feel, when they engage with you. It is what you bring to the party, or to a meeting, when you walk into a room, or when someone hears your voice at the end of the phone. How others perceive you, or 'sense' you, is often an unconscious reaction, a gut feeling, which does not always have a logical rationale.

What are you known for?

Are you known for your calm and measured approach to challenges, or does your mood swing from day-to-day, to the extent that people are unsure how to respond to you? Are you open and honest with others, or do you send out mixed messages? Are you recognised as the person who comes up with innovative solutions, or are you known for avoiding tough decisions?

We all have a personal brand, whether we consciously create it or not. You will dress in a certain way; perhaps you are very image-conscious, ensuring you are always immaculately presented, or maybe appearance is not that important to you.

Leaders who create a positive impact because of their personal brand, unconsciously influence the people around them - colleagues want to stay on their right side, and follow when they lead.
Your personal brand can influence and inspire those around you, to do more than is required; people will want to impress you, and some will work hard to obtain your acknowledgement and recognition.

Thomas

IT Manager, Thomas was frustrated. He had been with the same company for 5 years, having started off as a technical engineer. He had progressed slowly through the company over the years, and was now starting to apply for more senior roles. Although he often reached the final round of interviews, he still hadn't secured the senior role he felt he was ready for. Thomas was recommended for coaching to help improve his personal impact, as this was believed to be the reason he wasn't being selected for the top jobs.

On meeting Thomas, I could see that he was clearly an intelligent, personable and capable man, who knew his products well, and was passionate about developing technology for the organisation. By the end of our first meeting, I had uncovered some possible reasons for Thomas not progressing:

1. *Not promoting his achievements – although Thomas was driven by innovation and results, it wasn't in his nature to broadcast his achievements beyond his immediate department, and so those in the wider organisation were unaware of his contributions.*
2. *Poor networking skills – Thomas didn't see the point in networking; he disliked the thought that he should engage in small talk, and so avoided it whenever possible. This meant that he was an unknown quantity to many of his peers, and his reputation was blurred.*
3. *Physical appearance – Thomas was a large man, with a scruffy appearance.*

Thomas didn't have some of the key attributes that it took to be a senior leader, and he failed to make a positive impact when meeting new people. It was time to work with Thomas to develop his personal brand, and address some of the issues that were getting in the way.

Establish your credibility

Leaders who lack a clear positive personal brand have to work hard to be seen. They struggle to be noticed for interesting projects or promotion, and are often overlooked when advice is being sought. If you want to raise your profile, no-one else is going to do it on your behalf, you must stick your neck out, and let people know you are there. You need to demonstrate your knowledge, and establish your credibility. If you are one of the many who are reluctant to blow their own trumpet, stop for a moment, to consider what is preventing you from highlighting your successes? Is it because you were brought up not be big-headed, or is there a fear being perceived as a 'Smart Alec'?

Raising your profile is nothing to do with bragging, it is about **not** shying away from self-promotion, as long as this is done in a way which is authentic, which will benefit you, your team, and your organisation. If you are at the stage where you are preparing for your next career step, now is the time to establish your credibility, exhibit your expertise, and subtly let those who matter know that you deserve attention.

Thomas

Thomas was growing increasingly frustrated that his work achievements had not been recognised in the form of promotion. His confidence had been eroded through a series of rejections, and he didn't know how to build it up again, which was having a negative impact on his health and personal relationships. He was determined to do what was necessary to make some changes.

We explored the potential benefits of gaining promotion, and Thomas realised that it would give him greater self-esteem, confidence, and self-respect. Thomas was stuck in a loop, one that needed to be broken, so using some of the exercises from Chapter Two, we started to rebuild his confidence.

We explored his personal brand. Thomas was definitely not having the positive impact on those around him, to help him to progress. Despite wanting promotion, it seemed that Thomas was unconsciously sabotaging his chances. I helped Thomas to uncover several beliefs that were contributing to this behaviour. One of these was a belief that people who promoted their achievements were arrogant, so it was no surprise that Thomas preferred to keep his achievements under wraps.

Thomas wanted to be known for his creativity and innovation, but this would never happen if he didn't broadcast and share his ideas. Using a process similar to Exercise 2.2 in Chapter Two, Thomas decided to choose a more empowering belief that, "people who promote their achievements respect and value themselves". He started to share what he was working on, taking ownership for his ideas, and quietly promoting his successes.

Make yourself attractive to others

One of the keys to creating a positive personal impact, is to make yourself attractive to others. People who are regarded as being 'attractive' are perceived as being kinder, more talented, and more intelligent than others. This means that attractive people are more persuasive in terms of getting what they ask for, and influencing other people's behaviour. Being attractive is not about being good-looking or pretty, it is about coming across as confident, enthusiastic and optimistic about life.

Remember that when you lead a team, you become a role model to those around you; therefore be the kind of person that you would want to follow. You cannot hide when you are a leader. What you say, how you act, and how you respond to situations, will be noticed by those around you, influencing their behaviour and perception of you. Now is the time to start developing your personal brand. If you have not thought about your own personal brand before, try this exercise.

Exercise 3.1 - Your Personal Brand

- What kind of leader do you want to be perceived as? We have already covered this in finding the authentic 'you' as a leader when we looked at your values. You might want to revisit **Exercise 1.2 - Your Unique Set of Leadership Values** in Chapter One.
- What kind of image do you want to portray, and why?
- Your ideal image will be linked to your values. If being professional is important to you, then what do you need to do to come across as professional? This will involve how you look, how you talk, how you listen, and how you manage situations around you.
- What is important to you that you are known for? Do you want to be known for getting results, for being driven, for being tough but fair, for being an authentic leader?

Once you have decided what impact you want to have on others, you can start to check whether you are delivering this impact through your behaviour and your appearance.

Do you need to make a few changes? Note down your thoughts in your journal.

Persuasion and influence

The impact of your personal brand will be reflected in your ability to influence and persuade others. There is a subtle difference between *persuasion* and *influence*. When you are trying to persuade someone, you are deliberately trying to convince them to agree with you. To get them to change their behaviour, or to achieve a particular goal, you must consciously communicate what it is that you want, and why. It can be difficult to persuade someone to think and feel differently, when they have pre-conceived ideas.

Influencing someone has a more powerful impact, through creating trust and credibility. Influence arises when you have have earned respect, having built good relationships with those around you. When you develop more of the soft skills discussed throughout this book, you will find it much easier to influence others, as well as improving your persuasions skills.

Elizabeth Kuhnke in ***Persuasion and Influence for Dummies*** shares some tips and techniques for developing influence.

Top Tips - Expand your Influence

- Be clear about what you want.
- Respect the other person.
- Appeal to their values.
- State your proposal to meet their needs.
- Listen for feelings as well as content.
- Demonstrate empathy.
- Look for win/win outcomes.

2. COMMUNICATING YOUR BRAND

So how do you ensure that you make the right impact, so that you are perceived in the way you want to be? Well, the good news is that you have already made a start on this, by thinking about what kind of reputation you want to precede you, and the footprint you want to leave behind.

Your personal impact is largely influenced by how you communicate with other people. We communicate verbally and non-verbally, through our words, our tone, and our body language. Commonly-quoted statistics estimate that 55% of our communication is through our body language, 38% by the tone of our voice, and just 7% by the words that we use.

To demonstrate the impact of tone, imagine reading out loud a short paragraph from a book or magazine. If I asked you to read it with an 'aggressive' tone, it would come across very differently to you reading it with a 'cheerful' tone. The words are the same, but the tone communicates a very different message.

Non-verbal communication

Now imagine standing on stage, not saying a word. As you slowly cast your eyes over the audience, you stand tall and smile - what message are you giving out? However, if you stand there with your head down, looking at your feet, and wringing your hands, what does this posture portray? In both these examples, you are communicating to your audience without even opening your mouth. As soon as you walk into the room, it is the visual image that is unconsciously picked up and interpreted. Your non-verbal communication includes your body language, how you stand, what you do with your hands, eye contact, your smile, a grimace, how you sit, and even how you breathe. I think you are getting the picture!

When you walk into a meeting with a smile on your face, what impression are you giving to your team? They might be thinking; "great, he's in a good mood", or "there must be some positive news". Yet when you walk in with hunched shoulders, or with a frown on your face, your colleagues will brace themselves for bad news, or a dressing down.

Thomas

Because Thomas had been feeling de-motivated from the lack of recognition and promotion, he had become more withdrawn with his peers, and the senior management team.

Thomas realised that his lack of self-esteem was causing him to avoid eye contact, and he was not contributing to meetings as he used to. Upon reflection, Thomas noticed that he rarely smiled when he was in meetings, and his body language was so 'closed' that it was making him appear unapproachable. This alone was causing a great deal of damage to his reputation.

*To address this, I took Thomas through a powerful exercise where he could mentally rehearse how he would like to come across to his peers and the senior management team. Skip to Chapter Eight, Exercise **8.1 – Creating the Future**, to see an example of the process I used once he had adopted a more resourceful mindset.*

Feelings and thoughts affect physiology

How you feel inside will have a big impact on your physiology. If you are feeling anxious, you may be reluctant to make eye contact. You are less likely to be smiling, and there will be plenty of tell-tale signs before you even open your mouth. If you want to create the impression of a person with confidence, then you first need to feel and believe you are confident. Sometimes it can be difficult to convince yourself that you are confident when you do not feel it, so it is also possible to do this the other way round. If you want to feel confident, try 'acting as if' you actually are confident; adopt the posture of a confident person, and notice how this can generate positive feelings from the inside.

3. GROOMING

We have talked about how non-verbal communication is the most powerful part of how others perceive you, and we have discussed physiology. Now it is time to focus upon general appearance and grooming.

Can you remember meeting a new colleague who wore a shabby suit or scuffed shoes? Maybe a female colleague who had badly-bitten nails, unwashed hair or laddered tights. What was your first impression of them? We judge people all the time, so you will have unconsciously been making assumptions about them, because of their appearance.

When you meet someone for the first time, you quickly take in all aspects of them; how they look, what they are saying, and how they are saying it. You notice how they respond to you, whether they listen to what you are saying, and if they appear to know what they are talking about. All of this information is assessed in a split second, and the strongest, most foremost, impression, is what you see in front of you.

Pride in your appearance

You will have heard the saying "You don't get a second chance to make a first impression." What message does it give out if others do not take pride in their appearance? The extent to which appearance is important to you will depend on your values, and how you have been brought up.

Appearance is surprisingly important to me. I have noticed that when others do not make sufficient effort, then my judgement is either that they do not value and respect themselves, or they do not value and respect me. My belief is that if someone respects me, they will make an effort to look presentable for me. This is based upon my own values, which means that it is important to me to look professional when I have a client meeting, or to wear clothes that I know will be appropriate. If I am spending a day alone then I probably won't make such an effort, but I will still put some makeup on just in case the doorbell rings!

You probably will not know what another person's values are, or how important appearance is to them. However, I suggest you make the assumption that your colleagues and clients would rather you made an effort with your appearance, than not.

Thomas

Thomas is a large man, who often looked unkempt. His line manager confided in me that Thomas's appearance was one of the reasons holding him back from promotion, yet no-one in the organisation felt comfortable confronting the issue with Thomas for fear of upsetting him.

Because Thomas had been with the organisation for 5 years, it made it even more difficult to address. No-one had known how to raise the issue in the early days, and it had been brushed under the carpet, until it became obvious that it was holding back his career.

I explored this element of personal impact with Thomas. Of course he was aware of his size, but he had no idea that his appearance was preventing him from being promoted. In his mind, he was technically more than competent, and that he shouldn't be judged on his appearance. Thomas believed that he would never be able to look smart because of his size.

Once Thomas accepted that his appearance was holding him back, I suggested that he look for 'large' role models, men who were large, and yet looked smart. Thomas was surprised to find that there were plenty, and he engaged the help of an image consultant to help him find suits that flattered his figure, and to find colours that enhanced his skin tone. He also found a new barber, who managed to give him a much sharper hairstyle. The transformation was immediate, and he was pleasantly surprised to notice the reactions of people around him.

If you have not seen the 'make-over' programmes on TV, they are well worth watching to get hints and tips. You do not need to spend a lot of money, or have a model figure, to look smart and professional.

Once you have started making an effort to create a positive impact on those around you, you will begin to notice the effects your actions are having. Do people respond differently to you? Are they warmer towards you, more open to your ideas, more productive? Or have you frightened them off?! Notice what works, and what does not, and be flexible in trying out different approaches, until you feel you are getting the kind of response you want.

4. NETWORKING

If you are looking for promotion, then networking can benefit you in several ways. Firstly, it raises your profile. The more you circulate, the more others are aware of you, and you can let them know what you have been doing. It is also a good forum if you want to let others know that you are looking for a career move. Networking is good for developing existing relationships, making new contacts and looking for opportunities.

It always surprises me how many managers and senior leaders dislike 'networking'. Maybe this is because I find it easy, being an extrovert who enjoys meeting new people, and finding out about them. To me, it is like going to a party without the alcohol, and sometimes you do get a glass of wine thrown in as well.

What does the term 'networking' mean to you? If the thought of networking brings you out in a cold sweat, perhaps you perceive it to mean making small talk, having to worry about being entertaining, or you imagine being stuck with someone boring?

Consider the images that come to mind when you think about networking. If, like Thomas, you do not enjoy it, then most likely, it will be because you associate it with a previous negative experience. If you do not want to attend an event, your inner dialogue will already be negative, and of course, that will impact upon how you come across to others. A good start is to consider why networking is important to you, what are the benefits, and to explore ideas of how it can be fun and productive.

Now decide how you want to come across when you are networking. This is an exercise I used with Thomas.

Exercise 3.2 - Set your Networking Intention

Highlight the words that resonate with you, as you consider how you would like to be perceived. Alternatively, add your own:

Friendly	Polite	Intelligent
Knowledgeable	Approachable	Confident
Calm	Curious	Good listener
Entertaining	Good story teller	Professional
Articulate	Well informed	Well groomed

When you set the intention of how you want to be perceived, consider what you need to do, and what you can say to yourself to come across like this. Make a note in your journal.

I have found some common themes that contribute to people disliking networking, such as; who to talk to, what to say and how to escape! Here are some useful tips to address these specific concerns, and a few more.

Top Tips - Effective Networking

- Talk to someone who is stood on their own (they probably feel like you do.)
- Find a group of three. One person will be feeling left out.
- Avoid joining two people who are deep in conversation.
- Introduce yourself; 'Hi, I'm (insert your name here), do

you mind if I join you?'
- Ask questions about the other person. Prepare a mental list in advance.
- It's not the Spanish Inquisition. Ask a question, then listen.
- Be genuinely curious.
- Maintain eye contact, and smile when appropriate.
- Build rapport (we explore this later in the book.)
- Ensure there is a balance of them talking, and you talking.
- If you want to escape, politely break rapport (again, we will cover this later.)
- Look for others who appear lonely, catch their eye, and invite them into your 'group'.

You will find plenty more tips in **How to Talk to Anyone** by Leil Lowndes.

Thomas

When I first met Thomas, he didn't see the point in networking. He was resistant to the expectation that he 'should' engage in small talk, and so avoided it whenever possible. This meant that he was an unknown quantity to many of his peers, and his reputation was blurred.

I worked with Thomas to help him see the benefits of networking. Thomas realised that by getting to know his colleagues on a deeper level, they could get to know him better in return. He could share his ideas, and assess his colleague's reactions to them, on a more informal level. He also realised that networking could enhance his social life.

Thomas recognised that he had been closing himself off as a protection mechanism, to avoid rejection. However, this was now having the opposite effect - he was being rejected because he wasn't being visible, and he certainly wasn't being open.

With some tips, and new relationship-building techniques, Thomas began to accept invitations to networking events, and was surprised to find that he started to enjoy the interactions.

Within just a few months of completing the coaching programme, Thomas e-mailed me to say he had been successful in achieving his promotion, adding that his social circle was expanding, and he felt generally more confident and happy in himself.

In the spotlight

As you become more self-aware, you will start to notice the impact you are making when you are in the spotlight. It could be during your regular management meetings, during a performance review or when you are out networking, either with colleagues or clients. When you know the spotlight is on you, have you noticed how your self-talk goes into overdrive, and sometimes gets in the way of your natural behaviour?

Consider the last time you were in a meeting. No matter how experienced or knowledgeable you are, there will have been a certain amount of internal chatter going on.

"What will he think of me, if I say what I really think?"
"What if I'm asked a question I can't answer?"
"What if they object to my suggestions?"

All of these thoughts impact upon how you feel, how you feel impacts on your physiology and how you come across, even before you have opened your mouth. Can you remember walking into a meeting, and thinking to yourself: *"This is going to be a complete waste of time, I've got plenty other things I could be doing."*

Just having these thoughts will put you into a state of frustration, as you think about all the other things you could be doing, which means that your irritation will become more obvious than you realise. If you catch yourself feeling anxious or irritated, take notice of what you are focusing on, and change these thoughts to more empowering ones.

Monitor your personal impact

Promoting your personal brand will become second nature to you, as you continue to use these tools and techniques. Just as you learnt to drive a car, you will move from being consciously-incompetent, to unconsciously-competent. Do not wait for a special event to utilise these techniques, get into the habit of using them on a daily basis.

Notice the reactions of other people; try to guess the impact you are having on them, but be aware that you are only mind-reading, and will not know for sure. However, if you do notice you are doing something that is having a negative effect, consider what you can do differently to get a better result.

At the end of each day, ask yourself:
- Have you been consistent in your behaviour?
- What have you done to demonstrate your values?
- Have you followed through on your decisions?

If you are not sure what impact you are having on those around you, the simplest way of finding out is to ask. Be prepared for responses that you might not agree with, and consider whether you are prepared to do something about it. If you are serious about taking on a managerial or leadership role, then becoming aware of your personal brand, and promoting yourself, will enhance your chance of success.

Summary

1. Being perceived as attractive is not about being good looking, it is about being confident. Try **Exercise 3.1** to develop your 'attractiveness' through your own personal brand.
2. How you approach people, and day-to-day challenges, will influence the perception and the behaviour of those around you.
3. Raising your profile is not about bragging, it is about being proud of your achievements.
4. "You don't get a second chance to make a first impression".
5. Networking is great for making new contacts, looking for opportunities and building on existing relationships.
6. Review the **Networking Top Tips** to give you more confidence and make your networking more effective.
7. If you are not sure what impact you are having on those around you, the simplest way of finding out is to ask.

PART TWO

Your First 100 Days

CHAPTER FOUR

Engaging your New Team

"If your actions inspire others to dream more, learn more, do more and become more, you are a leader"

John Quincy Adams

Now that you have established the kind of leader you want to be, with strategies to adopt the most resourceful mindset and a clear personal brand, you are ready to step up to your first leadership role.

The first three months in your new position will be a crucial period, when your performance is being constantly assessed. You will experience a sense of urgency to deliver results as quickly as possible, without the luxury of a honeymoon period to settle in. This is the time to prove that your boss made the right decision in appointing you, and to demonstrate to your team that you deserve to be leading them.

There will be time pressures, with many practical, and emotional challenges to deal with. How well you prioritise and deal with these challenges will depend upon your range of soft skills - which will be enhanced as you work through the exercises in the book.

Your key responsibilities as a leader are to set a clear direction, to develop a high-performing team, and to deliver results. This is the time to set challenging goals, for both yourself and your team, which will ensure quick wins, especially ones which take you towards your first six or twelve month objectives.

Before we start to explore the direction you want to set for your new team or department, let us look at the people you have inherited, because getting the right team in place will be instrumental in helping you to deliver the required results.

1. YOUR NEW TEAM

If you are joining a new organisation, the team you are taking over will be an unknown quantity. Even if you are not new, having been promoted internally, it is important to gain an understanding of what you are taking on, and where you are starting from. This is not the time to lock yourself away. You want to show that, although you are leading the team, you are also part of it. Let them know that you are keen to understand what makes it tick, as well as rooting out any potential problems.

Who is reluctant to help you because they originally wanted your job? Is there someone looking to sabotage your success, and is there any 'deadwood' that needs to be dealt with? And you want to quickly discover who your allies and key influencers are.

It will be useful to discreetly explore the following questions from a variety of sources i.e. your peers, your new boss, your team members, and key clients or suppliers.

Exercise 4.1 - Team History

- Was your predecessor loved or loathed?
- What was their leadership style?
- What was the reason for their departure?
- How engaged were the team?
- Who are the key influencers?
- What does your new team think about your appointment?
- What is the history of the department?
- How has your department been perceived by others in the organisation until now?
- What are their expectations of you, and the team, now that you are at the helm?

During this phase you will be tapping into your observation and rapport-building skills, along with your finely-tuned listening skills, as you probe for more information. You will be making judgements and decisions based on the information gleaned, and using your communication skills to inform others.

You may find it helpful to first read **Chapter Six - Managing Relationships**, before embarking upon this research.

Build solid foundations

In this initial period, getting to know your team well will pay dividends. Spend some time with each team member to find out more about them, from a personal, as well as a professional, perspective. You are not looking to be their best friend, but you do want to be seen as approachable, and someone who cares about their well-being.

Consider the following questions, and weave them into daily conversations as you get to know the people who now report to you. This does not need to be a formal process.

Exercise 4.2 - Digging Deeper

- What are their specialist areas?
- What are their perceived strengths and weaknesses?
- Do they understand the importance of their role?
- What would make their role more worthwhile in their eyes?
- How do they feel they are progressing?
- What are their aspirations and ambitions?
- What are their challenges?
- What help do they need from you?
- Can you count on them to support you?

As you spend time with each team member, you will be building the foundations of a strong relationship, and finding out what is important to them. Meeting on a one-to-one basis will help each person feel valued, and significantly, be an important step for you, as you begin to put the building blocks in place to create an atmosphere of trust and openness.

Lorenzo

Lorenzo had recently taken on the post of CEO for an animal welfare charity, and felt that some of the team members he had inherited were resistant to his ideas for much-needed change. The team consisted of a mixture of volunteers and paid employees, some full-time but mainly part-time. His immediate direct reports, the Campaign Director and the Finance Director, were supportive of his ideas, but some of the more established team members were sceptical of Lorenzo and his vision to make the charity more 'business-like'. Lorenzo knew that he needed to gain the trust of the whole team, and had spent a day with them sharing his vision. Despite hearing words of approval on the day, behind the scenes he was still sensing a feeling of unrest.

Following our first coaching session, Lorenzo made the decision that he needed to sit down with each team member, even though his time was precious, and despite numerous other pressing demands. Over a period of two weeks, he spent an hour with each team member, simply asking questions, taking an interest in each person, listening to their concerns, and getting to know them. He was surprised to hear that no previous CEO had ever taken the time to sit with each person and find out about them. It was such a successful exercise that Lorenzo decided to schedule in half-hour meetings with each person, once a month, for the first six months.

> *This simple, but highly effective, exercise proved to be invaluable, both from a relationship-building perspective and a data/ideas-gathering exercise. It generated more ideas than Lorenzo had ever imagined, several of which were quickly implemented. The team were delighted to be acknowledged, and it opened a floodgate of further contributions.*

It may take some time for your new team to trust and respect you. They will need time to get to know you, to work out what your leadership style is, how you operate, and what your expectations are. The quicker you can get to know their personalities, strengths and motivations, and to get each team member on your side, the faster you can start delivering results.

Find out what is important to them, as individuals, and as a team. What support do they need from you to perform at their best? Listen to their concerns, and let them know that you are part of their team.

Keeping your friends

If you have been promoted internally, you may find yourself leading people who used to be not just your peers, but also good friends. The dynamics of this new working relationship are going to be different, so how do you handle this, now that you are no longer 'one of them'? Is it possible to maintain a friendship with someone who now reports to you? If they are a true friend, then they will want to support you and help you to succeed. After all, it is a two-way street, and they will want you to remain on their side as well.

Be decisive in setting out new boundaries, and, if necessary, clarify your new role and responsibilities, and how this might impact on your relationship. There may be times when you need to withhold or share sensitive information, and there may be times when you need to provide difficult feedback, but if handled with care, you should be able to deliver this in such a way that keeps your friendship intact. Whether you are in, or outside of, work there is no reason why you cannot maintain your friendship - it will just be different.

Stuck in the middle

When you take on your first management/leadership role, you will find that you are pulled and pushed from both above and below. You will have demands from your boss which need to be communicated 'downwards', and views from your team which need to be communicated 'upwards'. You must be able to communicate with, and to represent, both groups, changing your hat accordingly, whilst retaining authenticity and demonstrating your values.

To avoid being caught in the middle of these two groups, hold fast to your vision, your values and beliefs, and brush up on your relationship-building skills. Skip forward to Chapter Six to find out more about **Managing Relationships**.

2. SETTING A CLEAR DIRECTION

Your new team will be looking to you for direction. Staff will want to know what is expected of them, and how they fit into the bigger picture. Before you can start to clarify your vision, it is important that you fully understand the vision and mission of the organisation you work for - does it fit with your personal values? Are you passionate about your part in helping the company to succeed, and do you have a clear understanding of where you, and how your new team, fit into this organisational vision?

In your first few months, be courageous in how you define what it is that you want to achieve, and why. What is important to you, and your boss, that you achieve in the first six months? Consider how this will impact upon the company as a whole. The more energy, passion and conviction you put behind your vision, the more you will motivate your team to support you in achieving these company objectives.

As a new leader, there will be many demands on your time, therefore it is important to create a space in your busy schedule to be absolutely clear on where you are heading. Once you have this vision, supported by your values, expertise and passion, then your purpose will begin to feel truly authentic. If you do not yet have a clear vision, here is an exercise to get you started. It is a long exercise, so read through it all first before you begin.

Exercise 4.3 - Creating your Vision

Book a meeting with yourself. Allocate 30 – 60 minutes in your diary and find a meeting room, or close the door to your office. Move away from any potential distractions, i.e. your computer, Laptop or Tablet, and switch off your phone (turning it to silent is not enough, unless that also stops it vibrating!)

Now, project yourself forwards 1, 2 or 5 years, you choose the timescale. Let us imagine you have chosen 2 years, note what the date will be in 2 years time. What would you like to have happened by this date? What is your goal or outcome?

Use either the SMART process to clarify your goal, (Specific, Measurable, Agreed, Realistic, Time-bound), or a more engaging and motivating model, such as PRISM: Personal,

Realistic, Interesting, Specific, Measurable. Write out a few paragraphs to describe your outcome.

If the environment allows, move to another chair and, as you sit down, imagine that you are sitting down two years from now. As you sit in the 'chair of the future', write down the following statement:
It is (day/month/year) *and I am 'X'* (insert here what it is you want to have achieved).
State it in positive terms and in the present tense as if you have already achieved it.

As you reflect on what you have achieved, consider the following 'well-formed' questions and write down your responses:
1. Was the outcome within your control?
2. Why did you want this goal? What was important about achieving this?
3. Assuming that you have achieved your goal, notice:
- Where are you?
- What can you see?
- Who are you with?
- What are you doing?
- What does it feel like?
- What can you hear?
- What are you saying to yourself/to others?
4. What resources did you need to get it, both internal, and external resources i.e.
- Confidence, motivation, energy, persistence, drive
- Finances, training, knowledge, support team
5. How has achieving your goal affected other people?
- How did it benefit them?

- What were the risks?
6. In achieving your goal, did you lose, or significantly compromise anything as a result of your actions?
7. Was the outcome worth the cost and time it took, and was it in keeping with your values and beliefs?
8. Once you have answered all these questions, look back to the other chair, and imagine your younger self is sat in that chair.
9. What advice can you give to the younger you? What decisions did you make back then that helped you to achieve where you are now? Write down your responses.
10. When you are ready, move back to your original chair, and review the advice from the 'older' you.

What did you learn from this exercise? What advice do you need to take on board? Record your thoughts in your journal.

Your vision will now be taking shape. It should have ignited your passion, and have given you a clear purpose as to what you are aiming to achieve, both in your role with your team, and within the organisation. Does your vision feel authentic and genuine? Does it fit with your leadership values? Does it enable you to grow as a person, and to help those around you grow?

You will know when you have the right vision, as it will challenge, stimulate, and energise you. You will have total belief that you can achieve it, and, even if you are not exactly sure how, you will have the first few steps in mind.

Communicate your vision

Your vision is not going to materialise all on its own, although once you have written it down, and started to formulate a plan of how to get there, you will start to notice opportunities that you had not noticed before.

Now is the time to share and clearly communicate your vision to those around you. If your team does not know what you are aiming to achieve, how can they possibly know how they fit into the plan?

Be prepared for questions, and to be challenged. To be challenged is good – this will make you think carefully about your vision, and will help you to refine it, examining it from different perspectives. Retain a healthy flexibility, and demonstrate that you appreciate comments, and constructive input. An authentic leader empowers those around him, and so your vision will be benefitting others, not just yourself.

Define the milestones

Once you have communicated your vision and refined it, it is time to start building in the milestones. What are you aiming for in the first 12 months? Where do you need to be in six months' time? What are the specific actions to be taken that will help you achieve your outcomes? Remember your SMART goals – ensure that they are Specific, Measurable, Achievable, Realistic and Time-bound. Who will take responsibility for these actions? What are the time frames? What additional resources are necessary to ensure success? Keep your communication lines open, monitor progress regularly, and be flexible to change course if necessary.

Your team members will be more motivated when they can see how their specific responsibilities are relevant, worthwhile, and making a contribution to the bigger picture. Ensure that they know how important their role is, and acknowledge their successes along the way, both individually, and as a team. In your first few months, you will be looking for early wins, with measurable achievements, which demonstrate that both you and your team are delivering results.

3. ENGAGING YOUR TEAM

The extent of your leadership success will be reflected in how accomplished you are at engaging and motivating your team, therefore any time and effort spent developing employee engagement will be well-rewarded. Every leader should be striving to engage their team, because they are the ones who are going to help you deliver the required results. When employees are engaged, they have an emotional commitment to you, the organisation, it's vision, and it's values. This is different to 'employee satisfaction'. Engagement is demonstrated by employees who are fully-involved and enthusiastic about their work, which will make your job so much easier.

Encourage engagement

Fostering employee engagement is more than a quick pat on the back, and is rarely brought about by offering financial incentives. It is something which comes from within the individual, and your leadership skills will have a big impact on this. The stronger the relationships you have with those around you, the smarter and harder they will want to work for you.

Employees want to be well-informed about what is happening both in their team, and in the organisation. They need a forum to share their views, knowing that they will be respected and listened to. A recent study conducted by the Institute of Employment Studies (IES) concluded that the main driver of employee engagement is the sense of feeling valued and involved.

The main components include:
- An involvement in decision-making.
- The freedom to voice ideas which will be listened to.
- The opportunity to grow, and to be developed.
- Feeling that the organisation is concerned for the employees health and well-being.

The degree to which your team members are engaged, will be influenced by their job role, their responsibilities, and the experience they have whilst they are at work. Explore ways to empower them, and to demonstrate your trust. Show your appreciation and recognition for their efforts, but ensure that you hold them accountable. The way in which you act, respond, and communicate, will contribute significantly towards making their working day both meaningful and engaging.

Continue to create the time to find out what they are doing, and how they are progressing. Listen to, and act upon, their challenges and concerns. To explore more about motivating your team, read ***Gung Ho! How to Motivate People in any Organisation*** by Ken Blanchard and Sheldon Bowles.

Create a community

Feeling a valued part of a community is a basic human need, and a key component for feeling motivated. We thrive when we feel part of something larger that ourselves, and when our contribution is valued. Encourage collaboration wherever possible, and explore opportunities to promote teamwork.

Lorenzo

When Lorenzo started his new role, he sensed a lack of cohesion, and lack of community spirit. This was something he wanted to develop. He wondered whether it was due to the number of part-time staff. Lorenzo mentioned this when he had his one-to-one meetings with the team.

The feedback was that there had always been a 'them and us' atmosphere, where the management made the decisions, then dished out the decisions, and the direction. The rest of the team didn't feel involved in any decision-making process, and, historically, when they had put forward suggestions, they had either been rejected or were not followed through.

After some brainstorming, Lorenzo came up with the idea to create small committees for key areas of responsibility, starting with marketing, customer service, and fundraising. Each committee consisted of four team members, who would explore the issues within their area, and put forward suggestions for improvements. The management team would then carefully consider the suggestions, and approve any action where appropriate.

It's still early days, but there have been significant successes to date. Lorenzo has been impressed with the quality of ideas generated, and has already been able to implement several initiatives. The increase in team morale has been tangible.

Energy and enthusiasm

You are a role model for your team. When you arrive at work in the morning with energy, enthusiasm, and a positive attitude, your team

will pick up on this, and it will have a ripple effect.
When you follow through on your actions, this demonstrates your integrity, and that you 'walk the talk'. When you challenge behaviour that conflicts with your values, you will be respected, when you give feedback that is honest and delivered with respect, your reputation will be that of a strong leader.

Remember the saying "People don't leave organisations, they leave their boss". In my experience, this is absolutely true. Strong and authentic leaders hold on to their team members, they communicate effectively, set stretching and challenging targets, and show their appreciation accordingly.

Monitor progress

In the early days you will be full of good intentions, making a concerted effort to engage your team. But as your workload and responsibilities increase, it can be easy to take your eye off the ball, and assume everyone is as motivated as you are. It is crucial to monitor progress, solicit feedback, and ensure that each team member is as productive as they can be. Keep communication lines open, check in regularly, and ensure that you find time to celebrate and advertise the little wins, as well as the big ones.

Summary

1. The first three months of your new role are critical; this is when your behaviour, performance, and results are being judged.
2. Research the background of your new team from a variety of sources, to gauge where you stand. See **Exercise 4.1 - Team History** for suggested questions.
3. Remember Lorenzo's case study - time spent getting to know your team in this early period will pay huge dividends.
4. Make time to define your vision, and communicate it with

passion and conviction.
5. Ensure each team member is aware of how their role contributes to the achievement of the collective goals.
6. Constantly look for ways to engage your team – note what works, and do more of it.
7. Pay attention to what your team are doing, and how they are progressing. Take time to listen and help with their challenges and concerns.
8. Create an environment that shines with energy, enthusiasm, and positivity.
9. Remember: "People don't leave organisations, they leave their boss".

CHAPTER FIVE

Setting Expectations

"Our environment, the world in which we live and work, is a mirror of our attitudes and expectations"

Earl Nightingale

You are now starting to get a feel for your new team, what makes them tick and what is important to them. You are exploring what you need to do to engage those around you, and have an awareness of how your behaviour is impacting on the team's performance. You have also started to crystallise your vision of where you want to be in two years' time, and have considered the milestones which will act as stepping stones towards achieving this vision.

As you get the first few days and weeks of your new role under your belt, setting and managing expectations will be crucial to delivering results and achieving your goals.

Your success in your new role, and your career in general, will depend upon expectations; what you expect from those around you, other people's expectations of you, and indeed, your own self-imposed expectations. Whether planned or not, expectations will occur naturally. If they are not communicated, acknowledged, and thought carefully through by those involved, there are bound to be repercussions when they are not met.

1. MANAGING EXPECTATIONS

Because you have just been, or are about to be, appointed to your first leadership role, my assumption is that you will want to progress. If your new role is not clear from the beginning, how will you know what is expected of you, what the expected standard is, whether you are on the right track, or even worse, way off-track? How can you deliver the results expected of you in the time-frame required?

When mutual expectations are not agreed and not clearly communicated, the scene is set for confusion, embarrassment, disagreement, and ultimately conflict. As a human race we have a tendency to 'mind-read' and to make assumptions, second-guessing what others are thinking or feeling.

If you are being promoted internally to a more senior role then it may be assumed, rightly or wrongly, that you know what you are doing, and that you will shout out if you need help. If you are starting with a new organisation and coming from another senior role, it may be assumed that you are familiar with the unspoken 'rules' of a leadership team. Imagine turning up to a boardroom meeting, not knowing the usual protocol? If you did not know that it was common practice to arrive ten minutes early, then as you breeze in when the clock strikes 9am, all eyes will be on you, and your first boardroom meeting will be off to a bad start.

Communicate expectations

Lack of communication in organisations is a common complaint, from managers and team members alike. The majority of problems stem from sketchy and sporadic communication, and in particular, a failure to set and manage clear expectations.

It makes sense that expectations should be transparent right from the word 'Go'. If you are new to a leadership role, then this is the ideal time to decide what you expect from others, and to find out what is expected of you. If you have already been in your post for some time, and you recognise that your expectations are not being met, then perhaps it is time to do something about it.

Have you noticed that when you focus your attention on what you expect to get, you are far more likely to get it? If you expect resistance to a new idea, you will get resistance, but if you expect to hit your targets for the month (and take the necessary action of course), then you will hit your targets for the month.

I call this, the 'You get what you expect to get' approach. So, if you expect to find some useful tips and techniques in this book, then I am confident that you will find them!

Tracy

Tracy was feeling out of her depth. After five years in the marketing department, she had been internally promoted to Marketing Manager.

Tracy knew she had accumulated the skills and experience to manage the department, and had gathered plenty of ideas over time to improve systems and processes. She knew the team well, was aware of their strengths and weaknesses, and was confident that she could make a difference. However, a few weeks into the new role, Tracy's confidence started to evaporate.

After her first boardroom meeting Tracy was anxious that she was lacking 'an agenda'. She was unsure how to behave with her new peers, some of whom she had reported to in previous roles, and she was unsure what was expected of her from her boss, who had given her a blank canvas. Having been used to a lot of direction in her previous role, Tracy found this approach unsettling, and she desperately needed reassurance.

Despite feeling frustrated that she didn't know what was expected of her, Tracy was reluctant to share her concerns with her boss, not wanting to appear incapable of dealing with the issues herself, and keen to demonstrate that she was right for the job.

Make time to reflect

When you are new to a role, amidst the urgency to deliver results, being a manager or a leader can be a lonely place, not knowing who you can be open with, and who you can trust. However, no matter how frantic your working day might be, it is important to find time to reflect, and pay attention to the frustrations and concerns you are feeling, even if it is while eating your lunch, or journeying to work. If possible, share your thoughts with someone you know you can trust, and explore whether there are unclear expectations. If you do not have access to your own coach, then request or find yourself someone in the organisation who has had experience of a similar role and responsibilities, who you can touch base with, and use as a sounding board.

2. WHAT IS EXPECTED OF YOU?

What does your boss expect?

It is quite likely that your new boss has had a significant input in selecting and appointing you to your new role, so he is confident that you can deliver what is necessary to do the job. Your boss will no doubt have high expectations of you, and if you do well, it will reflect favourably on him.

Firstly, the most obvious expectations are tangible and practical ones - your job role, your detailed responsibilities, the hours that you work. You would be amazed at the number of leaders I meet who do not have a job description, particularly when promoted internally. There will also be the expectation that you deliver particular results, and that you act professionally. If your new boss expects you to manage certain situations which might fall outside of your job remit – do you know what these are? Are you expected to be available 24/7, are you expected to respond to e-mails in the evenings, or at weekends?

> ### Exercise 5.1 - Step into the Boss's Shoes
>
> An interesting exercise is to step into your boss's shoes for a moment. Imagine what it's like to be your boss.
> - What are their main concerns?
> - What are they trying to achieve?
> - What is important to them?
> - What do they want from you, above and beyond your job description?
> - Can you, and are you delivering on these areas?
>
> Jot down your responses in your journal.

Regardless of the list you have created containing what you **think** your boss wants from you, I suggest that you also have a conversation with him as soon as possible to find out for sure. When you have clear expectations from your boss, you will know exactly what you are aiming for, with no confusion, and no excuses for not delivering.

> ### Tracy
>
> *Tracy explained that she had never been given a job description, despite assurances that she would when she was first offered her promotion - no wonder she was struggling to get off the starting blocks. Her first action was to arrange a meeting with her boss, the Marketing Director, to clarify what was expected of her.*

Tracy prepared a list of questions to ensure that she knew exactly what she would be responsible for, including which decisions she could make herself, which needed to be approved by others, which meetings she was expected to attend, and what she was expected to contribute in those meetings. Tracy also needed to know what level of support she could expect from her boss.

If you are already in your new role, ask yourself whether your responsibilities have changed, but have not yet been verbalised? Are your targets clear and achievable? What information, or support, do you need from your boss to be more effective? When was the last time you had some honest feedback from him?

However busy you, or your boss are, the time invested in regular meetings will be well-rewarded. Discuss with your new boss how long, and how often, your meetings need to take place, perhaps once a week for an hour at first, when you are new to the role, changing to once a month as you settle in. Once you get into the habit of holding regular meetings with your boss, you will be able to manage each other's expectations, exploring any problems before they get out of hand, and there will be no hidden surprises when it comes to your annual performance review.

What does your team expect?

Your new team will also have high expectations of you. Your predecessor's leadership style will be an important determining factor, meaning you could have a tough act to follow if he was effective, or you could be welcomed with open arms if he was not. Nevertheless, if you are taking over from someone with a very different style, you will have to manage expectations quickly and carefully.

Team members tend to look for strong, decisive leadership, someone to help them develop their skills, empower and motivate them, to fight their corner and to help them progress. Of course these are just my assumptions based on many years of coaching managers and leaders, do you really know what your team expect from you?

Client expectations

Your company has worked hard to attract and develop its client base, making promises of what can be expected when dealing with you and your team. Client expectations will vary according to the specific organisation, industry sector, and culture, but if your role is client-facing, then high visibility, extensive product knowledge, and guaranteed delivery are likely to be demanded. Building relationships is the key to managing expectations - find out what is expected of you from your clients, and then communicate what they can expect from your service, the quality of your products, the availability of your team, and how you handle their requests. Your clients will feel more confident working with you.

You will also have 'internal clients'; other departments, stakeholders, and various groups of people within your organisation. What are their expectations of you and your team? How will you know whether you are delivering on their expectations?

When you are new to the organisation, a good place to start is to review the company's marketing material. Are you familiar with the company vision, its mission statement, and its core values? If these are not displayed on the company website, then you could be instrumental in exploring and clarifying what they are, depending on your role, and the size of the company.

An increasing number of organisations are now conducting customer, and employee surveys, to establish satisfaction levels, and to ensure that expectations are being met, and ideally exceeded. Is your organisation pro-active in this area, or do you sense that they are shying away from soliciting external or internal feedback? Asking questions is the best way to find out what other people are thinking about. Listen to their response and take the appropriate action to manage expectations.

3. CLARIFY YOUR OWN EXPECTATIONS

The organisation

At the most basic level, you will want your employer to pay you an agreed salary, perhaps an annual bonus, to provide you with a car or car allowance, and to offer you training and personal development.

Are your 'hygiene factors' being met? Hygiene factors are certain elements, or characteristics, of your job which you expect to receive. They will not necessarily motivate you, but they will certainly cause dissatisfaction if they are absent.

Exercise 5.2 - Hygiene Factors and Motivation

What is missing from this list of 'hygiene factors' that are important to you?
- Pleasant and appropriate working environment
- Expenses to be processed on time
- Security
- Pension
- What else?

When your hygiene factors have been met, what else do you

need, or expect, from your organisation to help you perform to the best of your ability, and to keep you motivated?
Some common motivators are recognition, achievement, progression, and responsibility. These will be tied in with your leadership values, and core values, which we explore later in this chapter.

What do you expect from your boss?

Your expectations of your boss will depend upon a number of factors; their reputation, your values, their leadership style, and your anticipated relationship with him, to name but a few. As a newly-appointed leader, your success, and that of your department, will depend on this crucial relationship, and how you communicate and manage each other's expectations.

Once again, consider what is important to you about the relationship with your boss, and how you expect to be treated, challenged, supported, and motivated. If you are already in your new role, are your expectations being met? If not, then when, where, and how, will you have the conversation to communicate your thoughts?

What do you expect from your team?

When you explore and discuss expectations with your new team, share your purpose, vision and goals with them. This way, they know what they are working towards, are clear as to what is expected of them, and understand how they fit in to the overall success of the team. Let them know what your core and leadership values are, and how this will be reflected in the behaviour and attitude you expect from them.

Procedural expectations are also important. Ensure that each team member is fully aware of their job role and responsibilities. They will require access to clear processes and procedures to assist them in completing their daily tasks, and to achieve their outcomes.

Although not always an easy task, it is up to you to explore ways of creating an inclusive and collaborative environment right from the beginning, so that expectations can be monitored and managed. This will encourage two-way communication and a greater commitment to helping you achieve your shared objectives. Individuals in your team will be more motivated to deal with challenges as they arise, becoming more creative and developing a greater sense of responsibility.

4. VALUES AND BELIEFS

Core values

We all have unconscious and unspoken expectations of what behaviour is, and is not, acceptable. You may naturally assume that your colleagues are honest, hardworking and trustworthy. Your unconscious expectations of others will generally be in alignment with your core values, these are the fundamental qualities which are most important to you. Your core values are a powerful set of criteria that underpin your actions and your decisions on a daily basis. They are what matters most to you, and will motivate you when met, but de-motivate you if not.

You will have other values which depend upon their context. Perhaps status is important to you at work, but not in a social situation, whilst fun may be important to you in your relationship, but not in your work role. However, your core values will stay with you across all contexts; they are the principles which you adhere to, day-by-day.

Conflicting values

We adopt our core values from those around us; our parents, teachers, friends, and colleagues. For example, if, when you were a child, you picked up from your parents that achieving high standards was important, then it will be important to you too. When your core values are not met or ignored, you may experience feelings of irritation, frustration, or dissatisfaction, which creates the ideal breeding ground for conflict, both internally and externally. When you understand your core values, it will start to make sense why certain people and certain behaviours frustrate you, and why you are not getting the results you want in life.

Exercise 5.3 - Uncover your Core Values

Find out what your core values are by trying this exercise. Read through this list of words and circle all the words that resonate with you, words or phrases that are important to you across all contexts of your life. Also consider what is important about how you are treated and how others treat you.

Abundance	Attentive	Be creative
Acceptance	Attract	Be joyful
Accomplish	Authenticity	Be passionate
Achieve	Balance	Be present
Acquire	Be accepted	Be sensitive
Adventure	Be accepting	Be spiritual
Articulate	Be active	Beauty
Artistic	Be amused	Bliss
Assemble	Be amusing	Bravery
Assist	Be aware	Build
Attain	Be connected	Calm

Candor	Elegance	Guide
Capable	Emphasise	Harmony
Challenge	Encourage	Health
Charisma	Endeavour	Helping others
Choice	Energise	Home Life
Coach	Energy	Honesty
Collaborate	Energy flow	Honour
Comfort	Enjoy	Humour
Communication	Enlighten	Imagination
Community	Entertain	Impact
Compassion	Environment	Improvement
Completion	Excellence	Independence
Conceive	Excitement	Influence
Congruent	Exhilaration	Inform
Connection	Experiment	Inquisitive
Consistency	Expert	Inspire
Contentment	Facilitate	Instruct
Control	Faith	Integrate
Courage	Fame	Integrity
Creativity	Family	Intelligence
Dare	Fortune	Intimacy
Dedication	Thinking	Invent
Delight	Freedom	Justice
Dependable	Friendship	Knowledge
Design	Fulfilment	Laugh
Direct	Fun	Leadership
Distinction	Gamble	Learn
Drama	Glamour	Leisure
Dream	Godliness	Love
Duty	Govern	Loyalty
Education	Grace	Inspire
Efficiency	Gratitude	Instruct

Integrate	Prestige	Travel
Integrity	Privacy	Triumph
Intelligence	Relationships	Trust
Intimacy	Religion	Trustworthy
Invent	Respect	Truth
Justice	Respond	Uncover
Knowledge	Routine	Open minded
Laugh	Rule	Orchestrate
Leadership	Satisfaction	Order
Learn	Security	Originality
Leisure	See	Partnership
Love	Seek	Passion
Loyalty	Self awareness	Radiance
Peace	Self esteem	Realise
People	Self expression	Recognition
Perception	Sensation	Refine
Perfection	Sense	Responsibility
Patient	Systems	Risk
Persevere	Team player	Space
Persuade	To risk	Speculate
Plan	To teach	Spirituality
Playful	To unite	Stability
Pleasure	To touch	Strength
Power	Touch	Success
Precision	Thought provoking	Wealth
Prepare	Transformation	Winning

When you have circled the words, or phrases that resonate with you, pare them down to just 20. Pare them down again until you have your ten most important ones, these will be your core values. In your journal, write a short description of what each word means to you, and **why** it is important to you.

Does your behaviour underpin and demonstrate these values? Does your professional role and organisation allow you to live by these values? If transparency is a core value, but you are encouraged to hide certain facts from customers, this will not sit comfortably with you, and will cause an inner conflict.

Tracy

As the coaching programme progressed, I helped Tracy to elicit her core values. As in the exercise above, we explored why each one was important and what the words meant to her. Included in Tracy's top ten values were: Recognition, Respect and Trust.

Here is what Tracy defined for Recognition:
Recognition means that I am acknowledged when I have done a good job. I am known and recognised by my peers and senior team for the skills I demonstrate and the results I achieve. Recognition is important to me because it makes me feel significant, and I know that the effort I put in is appreciated. It motivates me to want to do well. It feeds my confidence and self-esteem.

On reflection Tracy could see that her confidence and motivation levels had dipped shortly after she had started her new role because one of her core values – recognition - was not being fulfilled. By setting up a regular meeting with her new boss she was able to create an environment where she could share her progress and get the acknowledgment and recognition she needed.

Now that you know what your core values are, you could repeat a similar exercise with your new team, adding in words that may be important to the team, but are not listed above. Share and explore what is important to each of you. What underpinning values will be instrumental in your shared success? If you want to be able to manage the expectations that others have of you, make an effort to find out what is important to them, understand what this means to them and then, if appropriate, you can demonstrate the behaviour they are looking for. You do not have to have exactly the same values, but as long as you have mutual respect for each other's values, you will be amazed at how your relationships deepen.

Deep-seated beliefs

Unconscious expectations that you have of yourself and others will be underpinned by deep-seated beliefs which you have accumulated over the years. Your beliefs are your opinions. They are not generally fact, and are inextricably linked with your values. They are the foundation of what you think, say, feel, and do. As with your values, you will have picked up your beliefs from those around you - your parents, family members, teachers, friends, and colleagues.

We learn how to perform tasks at the conscious level, and then as we repeat these actions, they become unconscious behaviour. We do so many things without even thinking about them. When you open a door, do you consciously think about where to put your hand, or whether to pull or push? When you learnt to drive, do you remember how conscious you were of everything you did? As you became more proficient you did not have to think it through in such detail, and now you can drive to work without really knowing how you got there!

Beliefs from the past

We have already touched upon beliefs in Chapter Two. Your behaviour is determined by your beliefs and values, and when you raise your self-awareness of where these values and beliefs originated, you can begin to understand what drives your behaviour. Your beliefs are also influenced by past experiences. For example, if when you first started work, you were humiliated in a meeting when your idea was ridiculed, then your belief system might well be to keep quiet in meetings, because you are made fun of when you share your ideas. This may sound silly now, but such memories remain with us at the unconscious level.

Tracy

Careful questioning helped Tracy to uncover some deep-seated beliefs. She thought that if she asked for help, it would mean that she was incompetent at her job. She also believed that if she shared with her boss that she was feeling confused and lacking in confidence, then he would think less of her.

Once Tracy realised that these beliefs had come from a boss she had worked with in a previous company, and that she was mind-reading what her new boss would be thinking, I was able to help her to change these old beliefs. Tracy now believes that it is more productive to be open with her boss, and to use the support and resources available to her.

5. UNREALISTIC EXPECTATIONS

Let us explore how you can manage those obvious, and sometimes not so obvious, unrealistic expectations. There will be unrealistic targets that come from above and below. Those 'above' you who set the expectations will be constantly looking for increased productivity and better results, yet they might be out of touch with what is possible given the resources you have available. How do you question targets and expectations from a faceless board of directors?

Sometimes it may just feel impossible. You have been set tasks to accomplish and targets to achieve, and you must share these with your team. New managers and leaders often feel squeezed with the expectations from above, and squeezed by those from below. Your team need you to support them, you are doing your best to motivate and empower them, yet who is supporting you?

Challenging expectations

It can be difficult to question targets and expectations, and yet if you have looked at all the options and still see that these expectations are totally unrealistic, you must share your concerns with those who are generating them, and start looking for alternative solutions. If you do not feel comfortable challenging these expectations, stop for a moment and consider what could be causing this discomfort. Are there some deep-seated fears, or limiting beliefs lurking? Perhaps there is an old fear of sticking your neck out? Are you concerned about being perceived as not trying hard enough? Once you have identified the fear or belief, refer back to Chapter Two and complete **Exercise 2.2 - Changing your Beliefs**.

You have been chosen for your post because you have demonstrated leadership potential and I believe that you have all the inner resources you need to tackle this kind of situation. Take some time to reflect and remind yourself of your qualities and attributes, and the reasons why you believe you are capable of challenging these unrealistic expectations.

Exercise 5.4 - Risks and Benefits

Have you considered the risks and benefits of confronting the situation? Record your thoughts in your journal.

- If you share your concerns, what are the benefits?
- If you share your concerns, what are the risks?
- If you stay quiet what are the benefits?
- If you stay quiet what are the risks?

This awareness will help you to determine whether this is the right time to speak up, and to challenge these unrealistic expectations.

There is a certain amount of preparation required for this kind of conversation. You will need to gather all the facts, consider the outcome you are looking for and rehearse what you want to say. You will also need to pull on your inner resources to get you into the most positive and confident state of mind.

If you want to find out more about managing your emotions skip to Chapter Seven, and for more on how to handle difficult conversations jump ahead to Chapter Eight.

You have some strategies now to help you deal with unrealistic expectations. How will you notice when your team are struggling with the expectations you have imposed on them? Open communication is the key, keep talking, checking in with them, and ensuring they are on track. Be aware of signs of stress; if they are working too late, if they appear withdrawn, grumpy or tearful, then it is time for an open and honest chat.

Self-imposed expectations

To end this chapter, we will look at your own self-imposed expectations. These are the standards that we set ourselves, standards that are ingrained by our beliefs and values.

Do you expect that you should have in-depth knowledge about every aspect of your department? Do you believe that you should be able to step in and perform the jobs of each team member if absent? Do you believe you should arrive before everyone else in the morning, and be the last one to leave? Consider which self-imposed expectations may be holding you back, and decide whether you want to change it. It is your choice.

There will be many self-imposed expectations that serve you well. Consider the healthy expectations you have of yourself and acknowledge how these expectations help you to perform your role to the high standard that is expected.

When you become aware of both your expectations as well as those of others, and learn how to communicate and manage them, many of your frustrations and problems as a new leader will be considerably reduced.

Summary

1. Your success will be influenced by expectations, both your own, and those around you.
2. Take time to reflect upon and clarify your expectations.
3. Beware of making assumptions, you could be wrong.
4. Regular, honest, and open communication works wonders.
5. Your core values and beliefs underpin your behaviour, remember to complete **Exercise 5.3 - Uncover your Core Values**.
6. Ensure that your self-imposed expectations are realistic and motivating.
7. Be nice, be friendly, be yourself, but always remember that the best working relationships are based upon respect and trust, which are based upon actions and performance, not just words.
8. Prove yourself. Pitch in. Help out. Follow through. Meet every

commitment. '*Earn*' the respect and trust of others, and you will build truly rewarding relationships.

CHAPTER SIX
Managing Relationships

"The basic building block of good communications is the feeling that every human being is unique and of value."

Anon

Relating to people is core to your leadership role. You cannot be a successful leader without people wanting to follow you, and without support from those around you. For people to follow and support you, they must trust and respect you, and that is not going to happen overnight without some effort on your part in developing your communication skills.

You are communicating with people every day on some level. You might pass the time of day with the receptionist, have an in-depth conversation with one of your peers, give feedback to a team member, or pitch to a prospect. Are you aware of the impression you are having on these people and how that impression can potentially impact on your success? The better your relationship-building skills, the more positive an impact you will have on others, which in turn will contribute to your success as a leader.

Making connections

You will naturally be building relationships with those you come into contact with on a daily basis, your team members, peers, and admin staff. Of course some people will be more influential than others, and each relationship will be different, but if you want to maximise your impact and deliver results, you will need a supportive network of advocates around you. The receptionist, or a team member from another department, can be just as useful as a fellow manager. You do not need to be best friends with everyone, but when you make the effort to find out more about someone and make them feel important, they will want to help you because you make them feel good about themselves.

There is a big difference between briefly acknowledging someone first thing in the morning, and actively going out of your way to find out more about them. Do you remember a work colleague or boss who barely recognised your existence? How did you feel about them? How did you feel about yourself in their company? Did you feel ignored or insignificant, thinking to yourself *"I'm obviously not important"* or *"I must have done something to upset him"*? If so, you probably made up this story to explain the reason for being shunned. Consider, in light of this, how others might feel if you fail to acknowledge them.

If you are cold and aloof with your team, how are you going to get the most from them? How will you engage and motivate them? If you keep your distance from your boss, how will you know what makes him tick, and how will you be able to share your expertise, knowledge and successes with them? If you do not build a relationship with your client base, how will you know whether they are happy with your services?

To be a strong and effective leader, it is critical that you invest time and effort to build relationships with those you work with, demonstrating that you value each person you come into contact with.

Craig

Project Manager Craig was aware that his relationship with his boss James was deteriorating. Over the years, Craig and James had worked together as part of the same team, and recently James had been promoted to a more senior level. Craig now found himself reporting to James.

Craig was a hard worker and he got results - he had extensive knowledge of his industry sector, he managed his project team well, and he knew how to get the best from them. He was frustrated that James had achieved the promotion that Craig felt he deserved, and a rift had started to develop between the two of them. The problem was being brushed under the carpet by both parties.

Craig was feeling ignored and unappreciated. As a result he was reluctant to share his ideas with James, and he could see that James was not being proactive in helping him to further his career. In fact, Craig felt that James was trying to sabotage his progress. Needless to say, the situation was impacting on Craig's productivity, his contribution to projects, and his confidence. It was also affecting his reputation as he became aware that James was complaining about Craig's performance at a more senior level, but not addressing it directly with him.

1. THE BLOCKS TO BETTER RELATIONSHIPS

Many of the time-consuming and mind-consuming issues that clients bring to coaching, are the result of strained relationships. Poor working relationships affect motivation, creativity and productivity, and ultimately profit. There are various reasons for poor quality relationships; a lack of open and honest communication, a difference in values, cultures, or goals, contrasting personality styles, and different belief systems, to mention but a few. And of course, there are different expectations from all parties.

When we experience difficulties relating to another person, it is usually because there is some kind of flaw in our communication. Consider someone you are struggling to get on with.

- How do you see and feel about this other person?
- How do you see yourself when you are with them?
- How do you feel about yourself when you are with them?

How you relate to other people is generally based upon how you see and feel about yourself. This can be affected by how you feel about and see others, and what you are thinking about as a result of these perceptions. Your thoughts create your feelings, and your feelings drive your behaviour.

Mind-reading

When you start a new role, it is natural to wonder what your peers, your boss, and your new team think about you. Do they like you? Do they think you are competent? How are they comparing you to your predecessor? If you are feeling a little out of your depth, then this trail of thought can fuel the common fears of 'being found out', so beware! Fears are mostly made up from speculating and 'mind-reading' what we think to be the truth. With a lack of real evidence, it is easy to make up your own version of how you think others perceive you.

Are you guilty of mind-reading to explain another person's behaviour? If you are (and most of us are), then as soon as you realise that you are doing so, ask yourself, "What else might be the reason for them behaving in this way?", and keep asking yourself until you can come up with a list of positive reasons. You might never know the real reason, but it will certainly make you feel better.

Is it worth the effort?

If you are not already a keen relationship-builder, or you are very selective with whom you get to know, it could be because you fail to place enough importance on connecting with certain people. Maybe you do not believe that you should have to be the one to make an effort? If this sounds like you and there is someone you have been neglecting, consider what the benefits might be of building a deeper working relationship with this person. Keep pushing yourself until you have at least five good reasons.

Craig

I explained to Craig that he couldn't change James' behaviour, but he could change his own response to the situation. I asked him to list the benefits of actively building his work relationship with James. He had to dig deep, but finally came up with these responses:

- *To share ideas and knowledge*
- *Support each other better*
- *Share resources*
- *Reduced conflict between departments*
- *Better understanding of what's important to each other*
- *More harmonious atmosphere in the office*

Once Craig reviewed these tangible benefits, he was prepared to draw a line under the current situation, and start using his rapport-building skills, which we'll discuss in more detail later in the chapter.

Assumptions

Another factor that could be unconsciously getting in the way of your relationship-building is your belief system and what you assume to be true. These could include beliefs about yourself, how you should conduct yourself in your role, what you believe is appropriate behaviour, and who you believe you should be developing relationships with or not.

If you notice you are reluctant to build relationships with certain work colleagues, let's find out why and explore what you can do about it.

Exercise 6.1 - Uncovering Assumptions

What are you assuming to be true that is stopping you from actively building a relationship with this person? Keep asking yourself this question and write down the top five reasons here, or note them in your journal.

1. _____
2. _____
3. _____
4. _____
5. _____

You might find you have some answers like this:
- She won't be interested in what I have to say.
- I don't have time to build these relationships.
- I won't be respected if I am too friendly.
- He will think I'm after his job.

Once you have your list of assumptions, review these, and consider whether they are really relevant. Are these assumptions fact, beliefs, or are you guilty of mind-reading?

Beliefs are what you believe to be true, but not necessarily fact. Ask yourself how these beliefs are helping you - are they empowering you or limiting you? If you notice that some of these beliefs are limiting you, you can change them to be more empowering.

Let's take the example of 'limiting beliefs' from the previous list and change them into more empowering ones:
- I have knowledge and experience that I can share
- Building these relationships will free up more time for me

> - Getting to know my team will help us work more effectively together
> - We can share ideas and support each other
>
> Now review your own list and see how you can change these to more empowering beliefs. Record your new beliefs in your journal.

Once you have your list of positive, punchy new beliefs, you can refer to these on a daily basis to remind you of how relationship-building is helping you to succeed.

Beware comparisons

If one of your beliefs is that someone is more superior than you, and therefore would not be interested in talking to you, you have fallen into the common trap of comparing yourself to others, something we are all guilty of at one time or another. Are you comparing yourself to your predecessor, your peers, or your boss?

Comparing yourself to others can leave you feeling either inferior or superior. Both of these states can be destructive, because they create a false sense of who you really are and what you have to offer. When you stay centred and focus on your own skills, attributes, and achievements, you maintain a healthy self-respect, and can therefore appreciate what others have to offer, rather than feeling insecure because you are different.

2. FIRO THEORY

In the 1950's, Will Schutz created FIRO Theory (Fundamental Interpersonal Relations Orientation) during his quest to find out why some teams performed better than others under stressful conditions. The theory, and measuring instrument in the form of a questionnaire, explores the elements of Behaviour (Element B), Feelings (Element F), and Self-concept – how we see and feel about ourselves (Element S).

Research led Schutz to believe that underlying 'Behaviour', as detailed in FIRO Element B, there are three fundamental dimensions: Inclusion, Control and Openness. (In the original theory 'Openness' was termed 'Affection').

FIRO Element B explains why we behave as we do when we are in a group of people (a group can be two or more), and how our behaviour impacts on others. It helps us to understand some of the fundamental issues that arise from our interactions, and how our relationships influence the development of our self-concept. I find this theory fascinating as it explains some of the most common communication issues.

The three dimensions of FIRO Element B

1. **Inclusion** – the need to be involved, included, or recognised in relation to other people – am I 'in' or 'out'?
2. **Control** – the need to influence, to make decisions, to take responsibility, or take the lead – am I on the 'top' or the 'bottom'?
3. **Openness** – the need to share our innermost thoughts – am I 'open' or 'closed'?

We each have different levels of these needs i.e. to include others, or be included; to influence others, or to be influenced; to be open with others, or for others to be open with us. There is no right or wrong level. The important factor to note is how we respond when our needs are not met, and this will depend upon our level of self-esteem.

We have already discussed how our behaviour is driven by how we feel, by our values, and our beliefs. Most people's greatest fears are to be ignored, humiliated, or rejected, and the extent to which we experience these fears is based on how we see and feel about ourselves.

In the table below, you can see the type of activity that demonstrates each behaviour. When these behaviours and activities are both present, the results are positive feelings and empowering beliefs. When the behaviours are not met, it can unconsciously produce anxieties and fears.

Behaviour	Activity	Feeling	Belief	Anxiety	Fear
Inclusion	Involvement	Significant	I am valued	I am not valued	Being ignored
Control	Influence	Competent	I am capable	I am incapable	Being humiliated
Openness	Intimacy	Likeability	I am well liked	I am disliked	Being rejected

The healthier our self esteem is, the more rational and flexible we will be in response to our needs not being met, i.e. if I am not included or involved as much as I need to be, then it won't concern me.

If you *feel* confidently competent and capable of doing a good job, then you will tend to be more flexible in your need to take *control*, to make decisions or to influence others. If you are feeling *anxious*, as we all do at some stage, you may doubt your competence, driven by the unconscious *fear* of being shown up and being humiliated. This can drive you to micro-manage others at one extreme, or to abdicate responsibility at the other extreme.

Defensive behaviour

Consider the boss who micro-manages everything and everyone in the team. They have to be involved in everything, not allowing any room for creativity or for individual decisions. They are probably stressed with the responsibility, working all hours to watch over everybody and to monitor their every step. Leaders who micro-manage their teams are reluctant to delegate, because unconsciously they want to prove that they are indispensable. Or perhaps they also believe that their team is incompetent. Their greatest fear is usually about being 'found out', exposed that they do not know as much as they think they should. This is a classic example of low self-esteem (the value we put upon ourselves), as a result of poor self-concept (how we see ourselves).

Your need to take control could naturally be high or low (neither is right or wrong), but when you have a healthy self-concept, you allow yourself a greater flexibility about how much you need to direct, or make decisions for others. Because you accept yourself and value what you have to offer, you are happy to delegate and allow others to take control when the need arises.

Craig

Based on the information that Craig shared with me, it seemed that James was reluctant to lose control by allowing Craig to make important decisions. Since Craig was more than capable of making such decisions, having had more experience in certain areas of the business, it appeared that James was micro-managing Craig for fear of being exposed as less competent.

As I wasn't coaching James at the time, it was difficult to quantify this assumption or address the situation.

Observe those around you and see whether you can identify whether they have a high or low need for each of the three dimensions. If you have a low inclusion need, but some of your team members have high inclusion needs, then you will need to include them more. If they have low control needs, then they will need more direction from you.

To find out more about this fascinating theory I highly recommend Will Schutz's book, **The Human Element**.

Craig

As I continued to work with Craig, I observed how he interacted with other people, how he processed and shared his thoughts, and how he made his decisions. I also started to get a better impression of how his boss, James, conducted himself at work. Craig had an introverted style, preferring to think things through carefully, spending time alone to mull over ideas, concentrating on the facts and figures, paying great attention to detail.

James appeared to be an extrovert, preferring to talk through his ideas and share his concerns, getting his energy from being around groups of people, and finding out their thoughts. James was creative, a big-picture person, always looking for better ways of doing things, finding it easy to develop new strategies. Craig was more detailed, concentrating on the here and now, putting processes and procedures in place. James tended to make his decisions based upon how they would impact on the people around him, ensuring harmony, whilst Craig made his decisions based upon facts, and would make tough decisions, even if they were unpopular.

Even how the two men managed their world around them was different. Craig liked to know what was happening long-term, being good at planning and organising, with a structured approach to his work. James, on the other hand, was more responsive, looking out for new ideas and information, which he would happily incorporate into his plans.

James enjoyed flexibility, welcoming interruptions, but would start things and not always finish them. You can imagine how much this frustrated Craig. And you can imagine how frustrated James was with Craig's slow, methodical, and detailed approach, when all he really wanted was top-level information.

Once Craig became aware of how their different styles were affecting their relationship, he began to appreciate the positive aspects of these different styles and how they complemented each other. The challenge now was to communicate this new learning to James.

3. REPRESENTATIONAL SYSTEMS

Another reason for a lack of connection with others can be the result of having a different preferred 'representational system'.

We absorb information from around us using our five senses; sight, hearing, feeling, taste and smell. We process this data by recreating these senses in our mind, and so 'Re-presenting' the information and inwardly making sense of our experiences. Although most of us can use all the senses, we each have a preferred system for how we experience and perceive the world. You will typically have a preferred system of seeing (visual), hearing (auditory) or feeling (kinaesthetic). Whichever is your preferred system – or sense - you will tend to use this system more than the others.

Visual

The visual system creates our internal images; it is how we visualise, daydream, and see pictures in our mind's eye. People who have a visual preference will experience their world predominantly in pictures. They will still experience feelings and register what they have heard, because we experience life using a mixture of all the senses, but they will tend to notice images more prominently. You will recognise when someone has a visual preference because they talk very quickly. When they recount a story, they can see the pictures scrolling quickly across their mind, which means that they need to talk quickly to keep up with the pictures. You may notice that their eyes look upwards, darting from one side to the other.

Auditory

If your preferred representational system is auditory, you will be good at listening to the detail of what is being said, and you will find it easy to recount conversations almost word for word. Your eyes will move to the right and left level with your ears (depending on whether you are remembering a conversation, usually eyes left, or constructing one, usually eyes right). People with an auditory preference usually have a 'sing-song' voice, with lots of variation in their tone.

Kinaesthetic

If your preference is kinaesthetic, you will tend to be more tactile, to experience the world primarily through your feelings and emotions, whilst remaining sensitive to external stimuli. You may be more sensitive to how others feel, enjoy the texture of items, or pay more attention to your gut instinct. Your eyes will spend more time looking downwards, rather than up towards the sky. For most people, looking down to the left means you are having an internal chat with yourself, whilst looking down towards the right, means you are getting in touch with your emotions. People with a kinaesthetic preference tend to talk more slowly, as they need to get a feel for their words before saying them. Talking slowly like this may irritate a visual person, who is used to talking very quickly! Likewise, the quick-talking visual person will often frustrate a person with a kinaesthetic preference.

Language patterns

You may notice that people who have a stronger kinaesthetic preference use language such as: "I had a gut instinct about him", "It just didn't feel right" or "She was quite a cold person". Those with an auditory preference might say "We weren't on the same wavelength", "I hear what you're saying" or, "That sounds good".

Someone with a visual preference might say "I could see it wasn't going anywhere.", "It's clear to me", "Let me show you what I mean". You will find more examples later in this chapter.

Exercise 6.2 - Observing Preferences

Ask a friend to tell you about their first relationship break-up. When recalling a sad memory, the odds are that you may notice their eyes drop to the floor, and they will look to their right (your left). This would indicate that they are connecting with their emotions, and so have a kinaesthetic preference. Or if they are strongly visual, then their eyes will flick up to the left (your right) as they recall the images of that experience.

If they have an auditory preference, their eyes will stay level with their ears but they will be able to recount the story clearly and almost word for word as it happened.

You will notice that some people raise their eyes upwards to prevent tears, this can be so that they stop themselves getting too emotional.

Note the language they use, can you pick out which representational system they prefer?

Craig

Craig's preferred representational system was kinaesthetic, judging by the slow pace of his speech, his eye patterns and the phrases he used. After careful questioning about James, it seemed likely that James was highly visual, talking swiftly, and looking upwards when he was animated about a project. He would also use phrases such as 'I can see what you mean... it's clear to me... show me what you mean'. This difference in preferred representational systems was another important contributor to their communication challenges.

4. RAPPORT

Once you are aware of your own preferred representational system, and that of the other person, you can start to build rapport by matching their style. Quite often you will find that you are naturally in rapport with another person, it just 'clicks', and communication feels easy. However, when it is not natural, and you want to let the other person know that you are on the same wavelength, there are some simple techniques you can use.

Rapport is more than finding a common interest with the other person – although that is certainly a good place to start – it is the quality of a relationship that results in mutual trust and responsiveness.

People who are similar to each other tend to like each other. This is why we naturally look for commonalities when we first meet someone new. We are drawn to people who look like ourselves, dress in a similar way, talk like we do, or have similar jobs and values. But building rapport can be much more subtle and effective than this.

To create a deeper sense of connection, it is important to let the other person know that you understand and respect how they see their model of the world; i.e. you are able to 'speak their language'. When you do this, they will feel acknowledged, and will become more responsive towards you.

Building trust

Rapport can be built instantly, and over time this evolves into trust. Building rapport is at the heart of communication. There are three key ways in which we communicate:

- Body language.
- Tone.
- The words you use.

You can build rapport by matching and mirroring any of these three elements, although it is generally accepted that the most powerful element of communication, when face-to-face, is body language. If you are not convinced of this, try to imagine someone shaking their fist at you. You will have a pretty good idea of the message intended.

Body language

The most powerful and quickest way of building rapport therefore is to use similar body language to the other person. We are not talking about mimicking here, just subtly adopting a similar body position. If your boss is sat forward in his chair, then you could sit forward in your chair. If he has folded his arms, then you can fold your arms. This can be done quite discreetly.

We call this matching and mirroring. When you are matching, if your boss puts his right leg over his left knee, then you put your right leg over your left knee. If you are mirroring, then you do the reverse, so that you are a mirror image. Both are effective. Some people feel that actively building rapport using these techniques can be perceived as manipulative, and if you are not genuine in your reasons for building rapport, then this will come across in your behaviour. However, used for the correct reasons, it is a powerful tool.

Tone and tempo

You can also build rapport through speech, by adopting a similar tone, tempo, or pitch to the other person. Remember when I said that visual people tend to talk more quickly? If you have a kinaesthetic preference, then you will need to speed up your speech to build rapport. However, if you have a visual preference and the other person is kinaesthetic, then you will want to slow down.

Those people with an auditory preference tend to have sing-song voices, varying in pitch. You can practise adopting a similar tone, as long as you are not overtly mimicking them. That would come across as disrespectful, and you would be breaking rapport!

Matching words

As I mentioned earlier, each representational system has a preferred vocabulary of words, these are known as predicate phrases. If you notice someone has a more visual preference, they will tend to use visual words when in conversation, whereas if they are kinaesthetic, they will use more 'feeling' words.

If you can spot their preference, use their preferred words to build rapport. It is also helpful to repeat back some of the exact words and phrases used by the other person. This is different to paraphrasing, where you may misinterpret what is being said, and risk losing rapport. Here are some examples of sensory phrases and words.

Sensory phrases

Visual	Auditory	Kinaesthetic
I see what you mean	He's on the same wavelength	Get a grip
Look closely at this idea	It was humming with activity	I feel it in my bones
I have a hazy notion	That rings a bell	I'm under a lot of pressure
It's clear to me	You're not listening	You could feel the tension
Show me what you mean	I hear what you're saying	She's a cold woman
He's a shining example	We're in tune with each other	Let's keep in touch

Sensory words

Visual	Auditory	Kinaesthetic
appears	alarmed	catch
bright	describe	concrete
clarify	harmonise	feel
clear	hear	firm
eyeful	listen	grasp
focused	melody	handle
glimpse	note	hard
hazy	quiet	heated
imagine	silence	scrape
look	sound	sharp
paint	tell	smooth
see	told	solid
show	tuned	tap
visible	wavelength	touching

5. LISTENING SKILLS

One of the simplest and most effective ways of building rapport is to show a genuine interest in the other person. Listen with good eye contact, allow them time to answer your questions, and let them see your curiosity.

Many people admit to being poor listeners, for a variety of reasons. Here are a few common ones:
- We think, on average, four times faster than we speak. This means that when someone is talking to you, you can be having your own internal dialogue and drift off, merely pretending to listen.
- We make decisions very quickly as to whether the topic is important enough for us to pay attention. Therefore, if we decide at the outset it is not relevant or interesting enough, we switch off, merely nodding and smiling at the appropriate places.
- We switch off when ideas are too complicated or detailed, because we believe we will not be able to retain all the information.

There are five different levels of listening:
1. Listening with your ears – this is the most basic and most common level of attention, when you notice the words someone uses.
2. Listening with the inner ear – when you pick up the tone being used, how words are emphasised, and interpret the meaning behind the words.
3. Listening with your eyes – when you notice the other person's body language, and whether it is congruent with what they are saying.
4. Listening with your guts – when you pick up a sense of something, using instinct and intuition, even though it is not being overtly communicated.

5. Listening with your heart – this is the most powerful level, when you view a person with respect, acknowledging them for who they are as an individual, and when you are able to see their point of view. At this level, the other person will know that you are truly listening and paying attention.

Top Tips - Listen with your Heart

- Put the other person at ease, maintain eye contact while they are talking.
- Try to understand the other person's point of view, imagine standing in their shoes.
- Look out for facial gestures and body language; see if you can pick up what is not being said as well as what is being said.
- Reflect back what is being said to you, using their exact words, and check for clarification if you are unsure of the meaning or context.
- Avoid completing the other person's sentence. If they pause, allow them to continue when they are ready.
- Show genuine curiosity, and gently probe for more information.

The power of body language

We have already talked about body language, but this is worth repeating as it is so important. You can be saying the right words, at the right pace, with the right tone, but if your body language is wrong, particularly a lack of eye contact, then you will have lost the impact you want to make.

Exercise 6.3 - Rapport Building

Consider who you would like to have a better work relationship with. Just choose one person for the benefit of this exercise.

Over the next few days, see whether you can identify what their preferred representational system is. Notice the direction of their eyes when they talk, the language they use, and the speed they talk.

Start to build rapport with them, adopting a similar body language, match and mirror their tone and tempo when they talk, and use their preferred 'language'. Reflect back short phrases they use, as this indicates that you are listening to what they have said.

Notice how differently you feel about the relationship, and how the other person responds. You may not see changes immediately, so continue the exercise for a week or so, and record your observations.

I cannot promise that it will be plain sailing from here. Relationships need to be nurtured, and managed effectively as and when they go pear shaped. And they **will** go pear shaped at times, because we are human. Our behaviour fluctuates daily depending on what we are doing, who we are with, what we are feeling and thinking, what we have done, and what we are about to do.

You are not going to get on with everyone you meet. You will not like everyone, and not everyone is going to like you, no matter how hard you try to build rapport. But at least you can make the effort and you have some new skills to try out. Play with the techniques you are learning and see what works. If it works, do more of it. If you do not get on with someone, then you need to look at how, and what you are communicating. Did you know that you cannot NOT communicate?

Craig

Following my work with Craig, I spent some time working with James, and as far as I know they are still working together. Although they will never be best friends, they understand how their communication breakdown came about and are making a positive effort to work more effectively together.

They can now respect each other's qualities, appreciate how their styles complement each other and Craig has accepted that James has the right qualities for his senior role. The coaching process has helped Craig to broaden his leadership skills, and he is now preparing to apply for a more senior role.

6. MANAGING YOUR STAKEHOLDERS

As a new leader, it is critical to engage with, and get support from, your stakeholders. These are all the people who are affected by your work, anyone who has influence over it, or has in interest in its success. Managing your stakeholders will provide invaluable help and contribute to the successful completion of your projects. These could include individuals such as team members, fellow managers, clients, or the receptionist.

Exercise 6.4 - Define your Stakeholders

- Consider the key people with whom you need to build a relationship.
- Which category do they fall into: team members, board members, support staff, peers, or clients?
- Who else do you need to support you in achieving your tasks and goals?
- What will be the benefit of building relationships with each of these?
- Start to prioritise by considering: Who has the power to help or block you?
- Who has the most interest in your projects?
- What motivates them?
- Who is influenced by their decisions?

Record your responses in your journal.

There are many tools available on the internet to guide you through mapping out your key stakeholders and I can recommend ***Enemies & Advocates*** by Colin Gautrey. It is worth spending time to first analyse and prioritise your stakeholders, and then using the tools in this chapter to help you develop the soft skills needed to engage with them.

When you take the time to find out what makes people 'tick', respect their view of the world, and acknowledge their unique strengths, you will be building the foundations for healthy and productive working relationships.

Summary

1. Building and managing relationships quickly in the first few weeks of your new role is critical.
2. How you interact with others will depend on your own needs for inclusion, control and openness.
3. Value and respect the personality styles of those around you, refer back to Chapter One to refresh your memory on different personality styles.
4. Repeat **Exercise 6.3** on a weekly basis, selecting different people to build a better rapport with.
5. The most powerful and quickest way of building rapport is to use similar body language to the other person.
6. Listen with your heart, review the top tips to help you do this more often.
7. Define and manage your stakeholders, and they will provide invaluable help and contribute to the successful completion of your projects.

PART THREE

Day-to-Day Challenges

CHAPTER SEVEN

Exploring Emotions

"*Feelings are much like waves, we can't stop them from coming, but we can choose which one to surf.*"

Jonatan Martensson

We all experience emotions and exhibit them externally to varying degrees. Some people 'wear their heart upon their sleeves', whilst others are good at keeping their emotions well-hidden. As with all of our unconscious responses, our emotions exist for a reason. The key is to understand what is driving your emotions, and to ensure they are working for you, not against you.

There are three types of internally-generated feelings:
- Physiological feelings, i.e. thirst, hunger, sickness
- Emotional feelings, i.e. joy, sadness, fear, excitement
- Intuitive feelings, i.e. gut feeling, instinct

In this chapter we explore emotional feelings, these are your internal and external reactions to past, present, and future situations.

You will recognise common emotions such as happiness, anxiety, excitement, anger, love, and hate - each of these feelings will be reflected in your thoughts. For example, if you are feeling excited, then your thoughts will probably be focused on the anticipation that something good is going to happen. Likewise, if you are feeling anxious, you may be fearful that something unpleasant will happen. If you want to change how you feel, then you must change what you are thinking about.

Although your emotions are triggered by what you are thinking about, some thoughts, and therefore some emotional feelings, are habitual and unconscious. In order to change the feeling, you must become consciously aware of your thoughts, decide whether these thoughts are helping or hindering you, and decide what thoughts would be more empowering.

1. UNHELPFUL EMOTIONS

Being able to manage your emotions is a powerful skill, and essential for performing at your best. When I work with new managers and leaders, it is not unusual to discover negative emotions that are getting in the way of effective leadership competencies.

Once you understand the origin and purpose of negative emotions, and learn how to manage them, you will be able to replace them with positive emotions and feelings.

Guilt

A common, and often unhelpful, emotion is guilt. We generally feel guilty when we believe that we have done something wrong, or something that is perceived by others to be wrong. Maybe you had to make an unpopular decision, or gave feedback that upset someone.

A particularly common form of guilt is experienced by working mothers who are away from their young children for long hours. They take work home with them, or work unsociable hours, which means they are not spending quality time with their family.

As with all emotions, guilt has a positive intention, to remind you of your sense of right and wrong. You may feel guilty through habit, even though there is no need to feel guilty, but your unconscious mind is protecting you, preparing you for the backlash if you were to get found out, or should you make the wrong decision. The question is how to rationalise the guilty feeling; i.e. to accept it when it is relevant, and to let it go when it is not.

Exercise 7.1 - Your Guilt List

Make yourself a 'Guilt List' (for your eyes only of course!)
- When do you feel most guilty?
- What causes you to feel guilty?
- What do you think you have done 'wrong'?
- Who do you think is going to judge you?
- What is the purpose (positive reason) for feeling guilty?
- What would be a more empowering feeling or thought?

Is the purpose of your guilt to encourage you to leave the office earlier, and spend more time with your family? Or is it a guilt that comes from way back, from a comment made many years ago that you have held on to for all these years?

Record your responses in your journal.

Choosing to let go of guilt

If you are feeling guilty for a valid reason, then you can choose to do something about it. If you made a comment that upset a member of your team and feel bad about it, what do you need to do to resolve the issue?

Accept that you did something wrong, make the necessary amends, and let it go. The more you dwell on what has happened, the more it will play on your mind, and you still will not have resolved the issue. If your guilt is because you are leaving your child in a nursery for 8 hours a day, then remind yourself that you have options. You can either change your role, your working hours, or come to terms with the decision you have made.

Once again, notice how your guilt is fuelled by your thoughts. What could you choose to think about, and believe differently in order to let go of your guilt? If you are finding it difficult to let go of guilt, consider what might be stopping you from doing so.

Anger

If you believe that you have been offended or wronged in some way, your emotional response will be to feel angry - this can range from mild irritation to all-out rage. When you feel the anger well up inside you, it is an internal warning to tell you that something is wrong; a self-protection mechanism.

Anger generally manifests internally, with an elevated heart rate, increase in blood pressure, and a rush of adrenaline, very similar to the anxiety state, the unconscious mind goes into the 'Flight or Fight' mode. The resulting visible behaviour will depend on the intensity of the feeling - you will possibly turn red, clam up, shout out, or slam doors - but there will be a definite external indication that you are angry! Feeling angry does not have to be seen as negative. If handled correctly it can motivate you to be more assertive, to stand up for yourself, and to let others know that your values have been violated.

On the other hand, if you allow your anger to get out of control and become aggressive, it will be counterproductive and unhealthy.

Anger can become an unconscious and unwelcome habit. If it is not addressed effectively, it can lead to poor decision-making and ineffective problem solving, affecting your health, and creating problems with relationships at home and at work. However, if you are suppressing anger, this can be just as harmful as ranting and raving. Either way, anger places considerable stress on the body.

Sue

Area manager Sue was recommended for coaching to improve her personal impact. Sue's HR Manager explained that she had received complaints because Sue was loud and aggressive in meetings, often using foul language, and intimidating some of the senior leadership team around her.

Technically, Sue was highly competent and due for promotion, but her unprofessional conduct was holding her back. Although Sue had been with the organisation for several years, no-one had addressed the issue until a new Director was appointed.

When I met Sue, she was friendly, confident, and calm, but as we talked more about her role within the organisation her anger and frustration came to the surface. She was happy with her own team, but very frustrated by the lack of recognition and support from her peers and her old line manager.

As we touched on other areas in Sue's life, there seemed to be a pattern of being let down, not being taken seriously, and a lack of support, which resulted in Sue holding onto a lot of resentment and anger. She had developed a habit of venting this anger at work, which was manifesting itself as aggression. This was creating a negative impact on those around her.

Emotions rooted in the past

When you step back and rationalise a situation that is causing you frustration, it is not uncommon to find that the cause of the resulting anger originates from something that happened a long time ago. The source of negative emotions is often deeply rooted in the past. Maybe you were not allowed to express your feelings, or you felt insignificant. Perhaps you were humiliated or treated badly in a previous relationship. In those difficult situations, your unconscious mind will have responded with the 'flight or fight' mode.

Your unconscious mind hangs on to old memories, so that whenever it notices that you are approaching a similar situation that could put you in 'danger', it sounds an alarm – your heart starts pounding, your throat goes dry, and your mind goes blank. This is because your body has gone into protection mode and is sending all resources to your essential organs; blood pumps quickly around your body making your heart pound and ensures that your legs have the power they need to run, or your mind and mouth kicks into action to fight your corner!

Exercise 7.2 - Uncover the Triggers

The first step to addressing anger is to notice the triggers.
- What is it that makes your blood boil?
- Are you over-reacting, or is your anger valid?
- Keep a diary and make a note when you feel angry, rate its intensity on a scale of 1-10 (10 being very intense) and record the triggers.
- Note down the thoughts going through your mind as you experience the anger, what is it that you are focusing on?
- What do you need to think, say or do to enable you to let go of your anger?

Record your thoughts in your journal.

Sue

Sue had a good idea of what was triggering her frustration, but decided to keep a record of each time she felt angry over a two week period, using the questions in the exercise above.

She started to notice a pattern. Sue felt the angry when she was being ignored, when her suggestions were being overlooked, or when she wasn't included in decision-making meetings. Her inner dialogue was telling her that she wasn't important, and that her contribution wasn't being valued. Hence, her coping strategy was to shout loudly and aggressively so that she couldn't be ignored, reinforcing her unconscious belief that she must look and act strong in order to be respected. But this aggression was losing Sue the respect and the status that she craved.

Once Sue realised that she had a deep-seated belief of 'I'm not good enough', we were able to work on increasing her self-esteem, using similar exercises to those in Chapter Two.

In order to let go of anger, decide what state or feeling would be more empowering, and choose the appropriate thoughts and beliefs that will enable you to feel differently. This will help you to adopt a more assertive approach, which will give you the confidence to say what you think or feel, or to say what you need to say, while respecting yourself and respecting the other person.

Fear of being found out

"One day they will find me out." This is a phrase that I often hear when working with managers and senior leaders, a comment they wouldn't share readily with many people. Fear is an emotion

resulting from experiences in the past, or beliefs and assumptions about what might happen in the future.

Like other negative emotions, fear invokes a physical feeling that prepares you for a flight or fight response to a potentially negative outcome. There are different levels of fear, from mild anxiety to totally irrational reactions, i.e. a phobia.

Fearing that you might be exposed as incompetent could be the result of a rapid promotion, leaving you feeling out of your depth, or anxiety about not being able to deliver the results that you promised.

Feeling inadequate

What is the purpose of all these negative emotions? As already mentioned, all emotional feelings have a positive intention. As with other negative emotions, they are protecting you in some form; maybe the feelings of inadequacy are preparing you, should you fail to deliver? Remember that feelings of inadequacy come from thoughts of inadequacy, so pay attention to the thoughts going through your mind which trigger these feelings; "I'm not good enough, she/he is better than I am, I don't know everything I need to know".

Try to recall the first time that you felt inadequate or 'not good enough'? If you think back far enough, it was probably back in your childhood days; maybe your parents had high expectations and they showed their disappointment when you did not get a string of A's, maybe it was a comment from a teacher, or perhaps a conversation you overheard. If you picked up that other people had a low opinion of you, or were judging you harshly, (because as children we tend to believe what others tell us), you may have believed they were right. How you perceived yourself will have been affected as a result of these comments, and these memories will stay deep within you, until you get a different and more accurate perspective on them. When you start to feel inadequate, your behaviour will reflect this and, of course, you will be cautious about standing out, for fear of being humiliated.

Are your feelings still relevant?

Once you have found out where your feelings have come from, you can decide whether they are still relevant in the present day. Have your thoughts and beliefs have been holding you back? Consider whether you are willing to let go of these feelings of inadequacy. Acknowledge their purpose, and then make a conscious choice to let go of your old beliefs, and to change them to more empowering beliefs, using **Exercise 2.2 - Changing your Beliefs**.

If you are struggling to let go of negative emotions, I would strongly recommend that you find a professional counsellor or NLP Coach to help you.

Sue

Sue recognised that she was constantly trying to prove herself by setting tough goals and striving for recognition. As we explored the reason for this, it transpired that when Sue was at school, her teachers made comments which Sue interpreted as meaning she was 'ordinary', that she wouldn't amount to much, and the best she should expect would be a job stacking shelves in a supermarket.

Although Sue's reaction to these comments was to work hard and show that she would prove them wrong - which she did in bucket loads - she was still holding onto that old belief of inadequacy, and it was becoming a big problem. Once she understood what was driving her to constantly strive for bigger and better goals - her fear of being labelled 'ordinary', and how it was getting in the way of her success - she was able to let go of her old beliefs and start valuing what she had achieved. She was also able to let go of her anger, and we began working on developing her self-acceptance, which started to increase her self-confidence.

2. HARNESSING POSITIVE EMOTIONS

I have focused on negative emotions until now, because these will generally hamper your performance. They get in the way of how you communicate with others, how you react to certain situations, and affect how other people respond to you.

We have many positive emotions that serve us well, and it is helpful to be aware of these, and to harness the energy they can generate. As with negative emotions, positive emotions and feelings impact upon your behaviour, affecting your results. Think about a time when you were feeling especially happy with life - perhaps you had received some good news, or heard a particular song on the radio that reminded you of a great holiday. When you think about those times, you feel more upbeat, and walk with a spring in your step. You smile at people more, feel energetic and notice all the positive things around you. When you are feeling on top of the world, you are more proactive and positive, and you can deal with difficult situations more easily. This is an emotional feeling you will want to harness, and the next exercise will help you to do this.

Your baseline state

How you feel fluctuates daily, by the hour and sometimes more often. You will have a 'baseline state', which is your typical state of being. Do you generally have a sunny disposition or are you quite a serious person? Do you look on the bright side, or do you spend a lot of time worrying about what might happen? Whatever your baseline state, you mood will rise or dip depending on who you are with, what you have just done, or future events that you are anticipating.

Imagine receiving a phone call from an old friend (one you like!), inviting you to a party - you will smile and feel happy that your friend has got in touch. The next moment a member of your team hands in their notice. Your mood changes within an instant – you feel shocked, rejected, maybe disappointed, and start to worry about finding a replacement. You will recognise times when your internal state has changed quickly and in such a manner. This illustrates just how easily the way you feel can be impacted by external events and experiences.

Anchors

Can you remember your first day in your current position? How did you feel? Excited, anxious, or just keen to get started? In the same way that external events, people, smells, sounds and memories can change your internal state, so can your conscious thoughts. If you choose to, you can control how you feel inside. The internal and external events that trigger and change your mood are called 'anchors'.

Here is an exercise that will help you tap into positive feelings whenever you need to.

Exercise 7.3 - Set a Positive 'Anchor'

Try this exercise to build your confidence, or choose another empowering state/feeling you would like to develop.

1. Remember a time when you felt at your most confident (Or replace this with your required state).
2. Step back into that moment, and bring the picture to mind when you were feeling at your most confident.
3. Looking out through your own eyes, see what you saw, make sure it is in colour, introduce some movement. Make the picture life size and ensure that the colours bright and sharp.
4. Now recall what you are hearing as you remember this event, turn the volume up. Notice what you are saying, what others are saying to you, and notice what you are thinking as you feel at your most confident.
5. Feel how strong the confidence is growing, notice where you feel this in your body, and when you have got the confidence feeling as strong as you can, put your hand to that part of your body where you feel it.
6. Enjoy the feeling for 3 or 4 seconds, then let your hand drop down.
7. Wipe clear the screen of your mind.
8. Find another memory of having these confident feelings and repeat the exercise. Notice how the feeling is in the same location, make sure that you put your hand to the same part of your body to 'anchor in' each feeling of confidence. Do this twice more.
9. To test your 'anchor', step into the future and imagine you are making a presentation in a meeting. As you imagine walking into the meeting room, trigger the anchor by putting your hand on the place where you feel

> your confidence, and notice how differently you conduct yourself in this situation. Notice how your body language changes and your tone of voice reflects your confidence.

You can repeat this exercise with any positive feeling or state that you want to tap into. You might find it useful to set anchors for feeling relaxed (great for getting to sleep), energised, motivated, assertive, positive, or in control.

Sue

Sue decided that she wanted to develop a cocktail of feelings that would enable her to come across as calm, confident, and generate respect from those around the boardroom table. We created an anchor that contained experiences of when Sue felt quietly confident, calm, and respectful of those around her.

When Sue felt that she respected others, she was able to behave in a way that earned her the respect she felt she deserved.

3. STRESS

All of the negative emotions we explored earlier can contribute to stress. Whatever you perceive as the external factor or situation to be causing your stress, it is actually your reaction to it, and in particular your thoughts and subsequent feelings that create the stress in your body. These can commonly be feelings such as anxiety, guilt, anger, fear, disappointment, frustration, shame, overwhelm, inadequacy and depression.

A certain amount of stress is healthy and produces optimal performance, both mental and physical. We need stress to motivate us to get things done. In fact, not enough stress can be de-motivating, leading to lethargy, which in turn can create other problems.

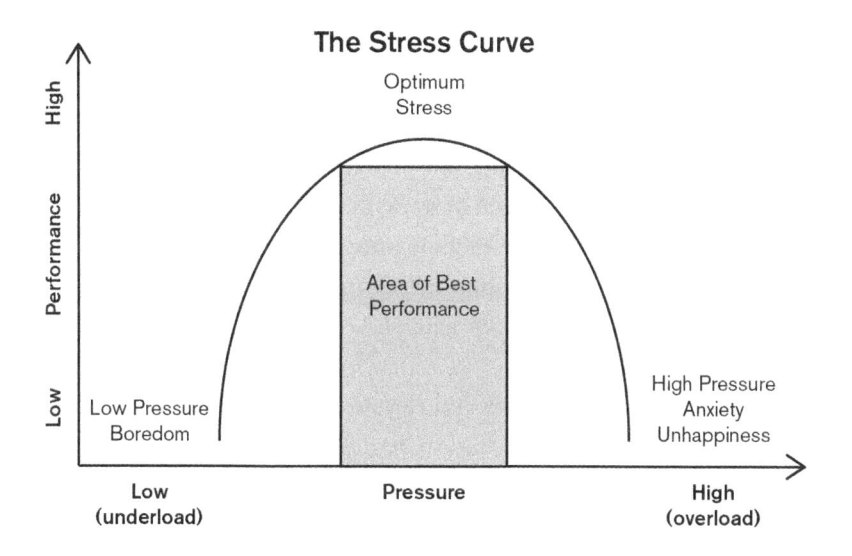

The Stress Curve

- Y-axis: Performance (Low to High)
- X-axis: Pressure (Low (underload) to High (overload))
- Optimum Stress / Area of Best Performance (middle)
- Low Pressure / Boredom (left)
- High Pressure / Anxiety / Unhappiness (right)

A healthy amount of stress helps you to stay focused - it gives you energy, purpose, keeps you alert, and can help you to rise to the challenge when extra motivation is needed. At the optimum level, you may feel stretched and challenged, and it is at this point that you achieve peak performance.

When you become overloaded, either physically or mentally, with too many activities and deadlines to cope with, you will move along the curve into the 'Stress zone', which triggers the familiar alarm bells of anxiety, panic, and for some people, anger or violence. This alarm is your unconscious mind protecting you, warning you to be careful. If these alarms are ignored, then the result is worry, interrupted sleep, underperformance, and even physical illness.

We all have different stress thresholds. Whilst one person is happy to be pushed and thrives on tight deadlines, this level of pressure may be unhealthy for someone else. You need to be aware of your limit, and the limits of those around you.

Causes of stress

Stress can be caused by both external and internal factors. External factors might include relationship difficulties with your boss or colleagues, financial problems, missing targets and deadlines, or simply having too much to achieve with insufficient resources or time. Internal factors might include unrealistic expectations of yourself and others, perfectionism, lack of self-belief, negative self-talk, or expecting the worst to happen.

Understanding what triggers and elevates your stress level will be useful in helping you to find strategies to cope. We tend to think that stress is caused by negative situations, yet events such as promotion at work, re-locating, or attending a conference, can also be very stressful for some.

What triggers cause your stress levels to rise?

Once you are aware of what is causing your stress levels to rise, you can choose to take action to minimise these situations. For example, if you feel stressed because you are always late for meetings, try to allow more time for travel, or plan to be in the meeting 10 minutes before the start, so that if you get held up you will still be there on time.

Sue

Sue found herself getting stressed and irritable because she was flying from one meeting to the next without any breathing space. Her diary was packed, and she quickly realised that meetings were being booked in by a new secretary who wasn't leaving her enough time to travel between meetings, let alone to make notes in between each one.

Sue allocated some time to meet with the secretary and set out boundaries to ensure that there was sufficient room in between meetings, so that Sue didn't have to break the speed limit to get there on time. This meant that she arrived at meetings prepared, and feeling calm and relaxed.

Review **your** stress triggers and make a note of what you can do to minimise these.

4. EMOTIONAL RESILIENCE

Many of your stress triggers will be part and parcel of your day-to-day activities. Stress levels rise as you are required to find solutions to problems, challenges, and manage the inevitable setbacks. There will be difficult situations and difficult people to handle, poor decisions, rejection, and disappointing results. There may be days when you feel de-motivated, low in energy, and your behaviour will reflect this. If you are struggling to deal with challenges and change, the resulting stress can have an impact on your performance, health and wellbeing, and will impact on those around you. As a leader, it is imperative that you learn how to manage your response to these situations. You will need to develop your emotional resilience.

What is emotional resilience?

Emotional resilience is the extent to how effectively you use your internal and external resources to respond to stressful situations or crises. It is how you 'bounce back', using a mixture of skills, habits, and outlooks, enabling you to remain flexible, creative, and alert in times of stress. Some people are more able to take things in their stride and adapt to situations with relative ease, while others find it more difficult.

Avoid the Blame Culture

So how can you build up your resilience muscles? In addition to having a good support team around you, and looking after yourself physically, how you manage your thoughts will have a major bearing on how emotionally resilient and flexible you are when faced with difficult situations. When things do not go according to plan, it is tempting to point the finger, and apportion blame elsewhere. I am sure we have all done it at some time, because it makes us feel better to blame someone else. Yet how is that really helping you? When you get into blame culture, your thoughts become negative, you feel negative, and you simply attract more negative situations to you. And, of course when you are feeling bad, your energy levels dip, motivation disappears, and it is all too much like hard work.

And if you are not blaming someone else, then you will get out the big stick and blame yourself for whatever has gone wrong. Neither of these approaches is helpful or productive, but you can get into a habit of reacting in this way. Now is the time to break the habit and understand how these unhelpful reactions are hindering your progress.

When was the last time you experienced a rejection or failure of some sort? What was your strategy for handling the situation?

What worked well, and what could you have done differently with hindsight? When you know what to do, you can become more resilient, even if you are naturally more sensitive to life's challenges.

Top Tips - Build your Emotional Resilience

1. Manage your thoughts. What are you focusing on?
2. Develop a 'can-do' attitude.
3. Develop your ability to manage and regulate your emotions.
4. Look for the positive in difficult situations.
5. Tap into your inner confidence.
6. Be as prepared as possible.
7. Build a strong network of supportive people around you.
8. Take responsibility for how you respond to situations that are outside of your control.
9. Emotional resilience needs energy – be aware of what energises you.
10. Look after your physical needs. Eat and drink healthily, exercise and get enough sleep.
11. Make time for fun and relaxation.
12. Use the techniques in this book to build your toolkit of coping strategies.

Handling De-motivation

Have you noticed that your emotional resilience tends to disappear when you feel de-motivated, and then your energy levels diminish? After many years of working with managers and leaders, I know that we all have periods of de-motivation, for a variety of reasons; not enough sleep, too much to do, not enough to do, uncertainty over abilities, or feeling threatened by others.

Motivation is a state of mind, and our internal state is driven by our thoughts. Can you see how the examples above have 'de-motivated thoughts' behind the reasons?

Causes of de-motivation

How do you know when you are de-motivated? For me, I am aware that I am not focused on the task at hand. I look for distractions, something that is easy to do, or anything that helps me avoid a complex task that requires my full attention.

John

John came for coaching because he was de-motivated at work, and was thinking of having a complete career change. When we got to the nub of the issue, John realised that his de-motivation was down to stress, work overload, plus a fear that new people were coming into the organisation with more knowledge than him and were nipping at his ankles, wanting to take his place.

Exercise 7.4 - Strategies for De-Motivation

Consider the following questions and record your thoughts in your journal.
- What is it like for you when you lack motivation?
- What happens?
- How do you feel inside?
- What do you see, and what do you say to yourself?
- When you are feeling de-motivated, do you know what your triggers are?

- Are they internal or external triggers?
- I am assuming that you are not constantly de-motivated, therefore you must be doing something to re-motivate yourself – what do you do?
- What is your strategy that works?

De-motivation can take hold when your emotional resilience is weak. Resilience to situations around you is an attitude, a belief, and a way of being. When you are resilient, you can handle what is thrown at you, look at it objectively, and make a decision on how to react. When you can look at the experience from a distance and remove the emotion, it becomes easier to learn from it and to find a strategy to help you for future situations.

John

Once John understood what was triggering his lack of motivation, and how it was impacting on his team around him, he felt a determination to do something about it, and he knew it was possible to make some changes.

We explored times when John had felt really motivated, what he was doing at the time, who was he with. He recalled conversations he was engaged in, what he was thinking about and what impact it was having. I asked John to imagine waking up the next day with 50% more motivation – and if I was following him around with a video camera, what would I see him doing differently?

John realised that he was more motivated when he was interacting with his team more, taking an interest in their progress, offering bits of advice and feeling more involved in the projects without getting too bogged down in the detail. He decided to re-introduce this behaviour into his daily routine when he went to the coffee machine, so that it felt easy and not a 'chore'. Just a small change has made a huge difference. John now feels more involved in what's happening, can offer input, he is learning from the others, and still has time to work at the strategic level.

5. MANAGING OTHER PEOPLE'S EMOTIONS

Working with other people and their respective emotions can be a minefield. As a strong leader and an effective team player, it is important to be aware of how others are feeling. Emotions are contagious. If there is someone in your team who is under stress, grumpy, de-motivated or even angry, then everyone else will know about it, and it can have an adverse effect on the whole team. At the very least it can be unsettling, and at worst, a major distraction.

We all have a duty of care to look out for others who might be struggling. When you are busy with your own tasks, targets, and challenges, you might not notice that a more introvert member of the team has become particularly quiet and uncommunicative.

Look out for telltale signs of stress in your team members. External signs that you might notice could include: being short tempered, indecisiveness, lack of concentration, lack of input in meetings, reluctance to take on new tasks, signs of tiredness, arriving late to work and unusual or regular absenteeism.

If you are busy yourself, what can you do to encourage members of your team to share their concerns, and to be open and honest with you? If they are struggling at home, or feeling overwhelmed at work, they might not want to admit that they cannot cope. How can you create an environment so that they can safely open up to you or someone in your team who can support them and help them to talk through their issues? There is a fine line between encouraging team members to share all their problems and bring home issues to work, and encouraging the right balance of openness. Some people are more open than others, some will need encouragement and some will need to be reigned in.

When to deal with issues

When you become aware that a team member or a colleague is exhibiting negative emotions, at what stage do you get involved? Do you step in immediately, or wait to see whether it resolves itself? This will become easier as you get to know your individual team members and colleagues. You will recognise those who are known to be 'drama queens', or whether they have a right to be annoyed or upset about something and you need to intervene.

Is the situation impacting on others in your team? Is it affecting the individual's performance, and importantly, could it be affecting their health? Again, it is a fine balance. If you step in too quickly, then you are setting expectations that you will always be there to sort out the problems, and your colleagues will not learn how to deal with them themselves.

When you become aware that other people around you are upset, stressed, or there is a conflict of some sort, the longer you consciously ignore it, the worse it may become. If you are hoping that it will sort itself out, give yourself a timeframe to check in with the situation, and make a decision at what stage to intervene.

What might stop you dealing with other people's emotions?

It would be easy to give you lots of advice as to what you **should** be doing to help resolve issues of team members and other colleagues. Consciously you probably already know what you should be doing, but in reality there may be deep-seated fears that may stop you from getting involved as early on as you could.

These underlying fears could include: not being sure how to deal with someone crying, shouting at you, accusing you, threatening you, walking out, raising a grievance, or generally feeling ill-equipped to handle the situation effectively and professionally. As always, these fears are driven by your thoughts, what has happened in previous situations, and what you expect might happen this time.

These are all genuine fears and concerns and will have come from past experience, whether it is something that happened to you personally, or something you have witnessed or heard about. As mentioned earlier, despite our fears having a positive intention, and being a self-protection mechanism, they are sometimes misguided and we simply need to draw on our inner resources, and sometimes external resources, to resolve the situation. So what you can do?

Strategies

The first step is to acknowledge what is going on. I would encourage conversations to be held in private, but it really depends on the situation. If it is a potential grievance, then of course the conversation must be recorded. Ensure that you set the boundaries for the discussion, clarify how much time is available, and set expectations for the meeting.

If there is more than one person involved then you must get the perspectives from each person. Use your listening skills, and ensure that you ask questions to establish the facts, as well as questions to explore possible solutions. Draw on your relationship-building skills, working towards establishing rapport, trust, and mutual respect. Be careful of being drawn into the situation, and maintain an objective perspective as far as is possible.

Before you help an emotional colleague, ensure that your emotions are in a positive and healthy state. Decide what state you need to be in to deal with the situation, i.e. calm, unbiased, in control, assertive. Tap into that state before you start the meeting and set yourself an empowering anchor, i.e. develop a calm or confident feeling, in advance if necessary. Refer back to **Exercise 7.3 – Set a Positive Anchor.**

Dealing with tears

Having to deal with tears is not uncommon, particularly when you take the time out really listen to someone's problems. In my experience, male leaders find it particularly difficult to handle a woman crying, and the tendency is to step in and comfort the other person. My advice is simply to acknowledge the tears, let them know it is OK, and offer a tissue. Crying is nothing to be ashamed of, and it can help someone let go of whatever they have been holding onto.

There will be times when you have had to deal with outbursts of emotion from other people, and there will certainly be times when you have handled the situations well. This is a good time to remember what has been successful in the past, and then apply this learning to your current situation.

Remember that you have external support too. If necessary talk to your HR department, or share your concerns with your peers and ask for their advice as to how they have dealt with similar situations.

When managed correctly, owning up to, and sharing emotions can be a powerful way of building relationships and making connections at a deeper level.

Summary

1. Your emotional feelings are generated by your thoughts.
2. If you feel guilty, decide whether it is relevant, and if not, decide to let it go.
3. Convert anger into healthy assertiveness.
4. Harness your positive emotions by reviewing **Exercise 7.3 - Set a Positive Anchor**.
5. Recognise your optimum level of stress.
6. Learn to look for the positive in challenging situations
7. Notice what strengthens your emotional resilience, and do more of it.
8. Before you handle someone else's emotions, ensure that your own are in a healthy state.

CHAPTER EIGHT

Handling Difficult Situations

"Difficulties are opportunities to better things; they are stepping-stones to greater experience… "

Brian Adams

Throughout your leadership role, it is inevitable that you will have difficult situations to handle. There will be situations that come from out of the blue, whilst others you might have seen coming. Some situations will be out of your control, others you may have created inadvertently. A difficult situation could range from dealing with an aggressive client, inter-department conflict, poor sales figures, or dealing with a grievance.

Challenges can also arise because of how we see and feel about the people involved in the situation, and how we see and feel about ourselves. Whatever kind of challenges you are faced with, they are all opportunities to learn and grow.

In this chapter I will talk about typical challenging situations that are often brought to coaching sessions, along with thoughts, tips and exercises to help you address some of them yourself.

1. DIFFICULT MEETINGS

A common theme that clients bring to coaching, is exploring effective ways to handle difficult meetings. The problem often manifests itself before even entering the meeting room, starting with a mental expectation of what is going to happen, what is expected of them, who will be present, and the unconscious anxiety about how they will be perceived.

If you are aiming to make a positive impact in a meeting, you must first consider the non-verbal elements of your communication. Starting with your appearance, are you dressed for the occasion? Do you look professional and well-groomed? Paying attention to your appearance, feeling proud of how you look forms the basis of how you see yourself, and will give you a greater sense of self-respect.

Manage your inner state

How do you want to feel as you enter the meeting? Do you want to feel calm, confident and in control for a board meeting, or relaxed and creative for a team brainstorming session? Or perhaps you want to feel prepared and assertive for a performance review? Once you know the most effective state required for a specific meeting, review **Exercise 7.3 – Set a Positive Anchor** in the previous chapter, and create a resourceful feeling that you can tap into when you require an extra boost.

Exercise 8.1 - Creating the Future

Now that you have a positive and resourceful state of mind, put an imaginary screen up on the wall and see yourself in the picture as you walk into the meeting room, or as you are sat in the meeting. Select the ideal image that works for you.
1. Visualise the meeting going exactly as you want it to go. How are you sitting? How does your body language reflect your desired state?
2. Notice what is different as you speak - how do you sound? Is your voice strong, clear, calm, and confident?
3. Now, step into this picture, and note how you feel, with everything going as planned.
4. Notice the reaction you are getting from those around you.
5. What thoughts are going through you mind now? Is there anything you need to change in the picture to make the meeting happen exactly as you would like it to?

Jot down your thoughts in your journal, noting how it feels when you are at your most confident. Notice your posture, and how you are talking.

> Once you have mentally rehearsed how you want your meeting to evolve, you are well on your way to ensuring the meeting will happen, just as you imagined it would.

Gerry

Gerry would often find himself losing confidence in a meeting as he began to muse whether people were really listening to him, and second guess what they were thinking. In mid conversation, his internal dialogue would get so loud that it would interrupt his line of thought, and he would forget what he supposed to be saying. This ended up with him mumbling, and not getting his main point across.

As I worked with Gerry, he was able to recognise that the inner voice was trying to assist him. It was helping him to evaluate other people's reactions, so that he could adapt his message as necessary. He was frustrated that it wasn't really helping him though, and wanted to find some way of quietening it down, without shutting it up completely.

Gerry decided that it would help to turn down the volume. He had an image of a large dial on an old-fashioned radio, and as he turned the dial round, the volume of his inner dialogue decreased. He managed to get the 'inner voice' down to a whisper, and that allowed him to bring in another more empowering voice, which suggested he focus on the task in hand, and he could then trigger his confidence anchor. This 'anchor' placed him back on track and returned him back to a more resourceful state.

Meeting preparation

When working with clients to improve their handling of difficult meetings, a lack of preparation is a common cause I encounter. Even though at a conscious level managers know that this will help, other priorities take over, time runs out and they just do not get round to preparing sufficiently.

Stop and consider for a moment; how would you benefit by taking more time to prepare? The time required will depend upon what kind of meeting it is. Sometimes it will involve some quick, mental preparation to get into the right state of mind, whilst at other times it can be as lengthy as preparing a full presentation.

A mental rehearsal of the meeting (see **Exercise 8.1 – Creating the Future**) will get you into the right state of mind, ensuring that you have already considered your appearance and posture. Where you sit in the meeting might be out of your control, but if you do have a choice, determine where the best place would be, and whether you need to arrive early to secure your ideal seat.

What is within your control?

Now imagine that you are in the meeting. You are in the right mental space, you feel confident, you have prepared as much as possible, and you know that you have a valuable contribution to make. You have taken control of as much as you can, yet there is still a great deal outside of your control.

You cannot change the behaviour of other people in the meeting, and maybe you cannot control what is being discussed or decided. However, you **can** control how you respond to situations that you see as problematic for you personally, or for your department. When something happens in the meeting that you perceive to be a problem, directed at you or your team, how you handle it will impact upon how effectively you can manage and minimise the issue. The first step is to maintain your confident state of mind. If you have been completing the exercises so far, you will have one or two 'resource anchors' (positive feelings) that you can trigger. As long as you are feeling calm, confident, and in control, you will generally be able to respond effectively.

Take responsibility

If it is necessary to do so, acknowledge, and admit to your mistakes. Accept the situation with respect, and focus on what the solution could be, or what steps you might take to address the situation. If the temptation is to get angry, or if your emotions are about to overrule you, it will be necessary to recall your resource anchor. The key is to maintain respect for yourself, and respect for those around you. Hold onto your state of confidence, assimilate the facts, speak up for yourself, and take responsibility for ensuring the necessary action is taken.

There might be times when you need additional external resources, which is fine – simply ask for help; there is no shame in requesting the use of resources around you.

2. DIFFICULT CONVERSATIONS

Difficult situations will usually include difficult conversations, and because they are perceived to be difficult, we tend to put them off. Difficult conversations might include rejecting a proposal, undertaking a challenging performance review, or advising of redundancies. And there will be plenty others in between.

Let us explore what might be stopping you from tackling them head on.

Exercise 8.2 - Avoidance Themes

1. Make a list of the difficult conversations you 'should' or could be having in the next few days or weeks. Think about situations outside of work as well as at work, and if you can, note down at least five conversations.
2. Against each conversation, make a note of what is stopping you from saying what you need to say.
3. Are you noticing a theme? If you have at least five examples, and five reasons for not addressing them, there may be an obvious theme.

Fear – the common cause

For many people, a common avoidance factor is fear. Fear of upsetting the other person, fear of not being able to handle their response, fear of rejection, fear of being perceived as heavy-handed, arrogant or uncaring. A lot of these fears will be unnecessary and are almost always a result of mind-reading. Some may be based on something that happened a long time ago and is not relevant any more. Consider what your 'fears' are, make a list of them, and decide whether they are substantiated in any way.

Exercise 8.3 - Courage, and the Pros and Cons

In order for you to overcome your fears, you will need courage. Think about previous experiences when you have had to deal with difficult conversations in the past, particularly times when you dealt with them well.
- What did you do?

- What resources did you draw upon?

Make a list of your strengths, and your strategy for finding the courage you need in difficult situations.

The next step is to uncover the risks and benefits of having, or not having, the conversation.

Take one of your anticipated conversations from your earlier list, and consider the next few questions.

Write down in your journal your responses as this will have a stronger impact for you.

1. If you have the conversation, what will it give you?
2. If you have the conversation, what won't it give you?
3. If you don't have the conversation, what will it give you?
4. If you don't have the conversation, what won't it give you?

These questions will help you clarify your thoughts, and help you to make a more informed decision. They will either motivate you, giving you courage to say what you need to say, or they will give you the permission you require to let it go.

When is the right time?

Choosing the right time and location is an important factor when you are planning to instigate or conduct a difficult conversation, particularly if this is within your control. If you are due to give some bad news to a team member, for example putting them on a Performance Improvement Plan, then telling them this news on a Friday afternoon is not good timing. They will need your support in the immediate days that follow, and it is unfair to spoil their weekend.

Whatever the conversation, consider a location that will help build and maintain rapport, put the other person/people at ease, and contribute to the flow of the meeting. Decide what outcome you desire to help you determine the best location. If you are dealing with a grievance procedure, you might want to be in the boardroom or in the HR department. If it is a more personal conversation, you might want to take them to lunch or for a coffee, ensuring that you have some private space.

Set your intention

As with preparing for meetings, it will help if you mentally set your intention for the conversation. What do you want the outcome to be? What do you need to cover? What questions or comments can you anticipate so that you are prepared with possible responses?

One of the keys to managing a difficult conversation effectively, and to get the result you want, is to ensure that you have a good rapport with the other party at all times. If you deliver the message with respect for the other person, even if the news is unpleasant or unwelcome, then you will soften the impact. Review **Chapter Six – Managing Relationships**, and remember that there are many ways to build and maintain rapport. As Milton Erikkson said, *"Anything is possible in the presence of rapport"*.

Top Tips - Handling Difficult People

1. Adopt similar body language and maintain eye contact.
2. Listen and respond with respect.
3. Reflect back words and phrases used by the other person to demonstrate that you have acknowledged them.
4. Use a similar tone and tempo.

5. Note whether they have a visual, auditory or kinaesthetic preference, and use the relevant words.
6. Avoid using the word **BUT** after giving positive feedback, it will delete all the positive words preceding it. Use **AND** instead.
7. Take a non-judgemental, non-critical approach.

Notice your emotions

Once again, it is important to monitor your internal state, and be aware of the emotions you are feeling as you have the conversation. Sometimes things might get heated and you may be tempted to respond in kind, perhaps with anger, frustration, or even guilt. As soon as you feel you are losing control of the situation, pause, notice the emotion you are feeling, locate it, and take three deep breaths.

Trigger an appropriate resource anchor - you will have a few by now if you have been following the exercises in the book - and continue with the conversation.

Share how you are feeling with the other person, as this will give them permission to share how they are feeling too. Be careful not to accuse someone else of "making me feel ..." No-one else can make you feel anything, you choose your own feelings, whether it is a conscious or unconscious decision.

Take the time to reflect on a difficult conversation that has gone well, and make a mental note of what you did to facilitate that conversation. You will start to build up a repository of strategies that work, and this will give you extra confidence and courage. For more strategies on this topic, read ***Fierce Conversations*** by Susan Scott.

Julie

Julie, a senior Executive Search Consultant, was frustrated with one of her clients. The client had interviewed several excellent candidates, but each time the position had been offered, the preferred candidate had turned the job down.

During a conversation with one of the candidates, Julie discovered that her client had arrived late for the interview, was inappropriately dressed, and had taken phone calls throughout the interview. The candidate had felt unable to work with such an unprofessional person. Further discussions with other candidates revealed a similar theme. Julie knew that she had to relay the feedback to her client, but was afraid of offending him and losing the business.

I worked with Julie to help her uncover the benefits and risks of having a direct and honest conversation with her client. Clearly there were risks in giving honest feedback, but the benefits far outweighed the risk of not saying anything. Julie imagined herself in the place of her client - what would his reaction be to receiving some honest feedback as to why he could not fill his vacancy?

With the help of a resource anchor to give her a positive mindset to tap into, Julie had the long-overdue feedback meeting with her client. At first he was stunned by her directness, but because she had spent time building rapport him, he took her comments onboard, and was immensely grateful for her honesty. He promised to change his behaviour and, shortly afterwards, filled the post with one of Julie's candidates.

3. HANDLING CONFLICT

When people are interacting with each other, there are bound to be conflict situations. This might be between yourself and another person, or between two people in your team. There could be conflict between various people, but let us focus on your team, because for you to be an effective leader you will need to be able to resolve these issues quickly, otherwise they will become very time-consuming.

Conflict arises for many reasons, most commonly when the two parties involved have different sets of values, or are working towards different goals. As we have already seen, conflict can also be exacerbated by different personality styles, different representational systems, and other factors, such as cultural differences.

As soon as you are aware of conflict, whether between yourself and someone else, or between two other people in your team, it needs to be nipped in the bud. Sounds obvious, so why are so many Human Resources departments kept busy with grievances and disciplinary actions?

We are very good at avoiding conflict because we do not like confrontation, and we are sensitive to offending other people. Handling conflict is a huge topic, and for the purposes of this book I am going to keep this relatively simple with a few tips.

Top Tips - Dealing with Conflict

1. Find out what is going on – speak to both parties involved – and gather information.
2. Listen carefully, respecting their model of the world.

3. Find out what is important to each party.
4. Find out what each party wants to achieve.
5. Encourage them to come up with their own solutions to the dilemma.
6. Use the interpersonal skills you are developing as you read this book.

Honest feedback

Relationships work best when you are open and honest with those around you. Yes, you need to be tactful and pick the right time to have a difficult conversation, but there will be times when you need to give constructive feedback to a team member, when either their performance or their behaviour is unacceptable.

To avoid giving feedback can be as damaging as avoiding conflict. In fact, the thought of giving feedback, particularly 'constructive' feedback is often perceived as conflict, so it is no wonder we shy away from it.

If you avoid giving feedback to a team member because their performance is not up to scratch or you don't like the way they are handling something, then how will they know that you are unhappy? How will they know that they are not achieving the expected standard, and therefore how can they do something about it?

When you deliver feedback in the appropriate way, then you are setting and managing expectations, therefore demonstrating the skills of a strong leader. If you fail to keep your team member on the right track as soon as you notice discrepancies, then they will continue to go further off-track, and assume it is acceptable to do so.

Make time to prepare

If you want to maintain good relationships, then the approach you take to giving feedback is crucial. Relationships can be easily damaged if you fail to carefully think through the intended message, the words which should be used, and the way in which you say them.

Before you start to give feedback, consider:
- What is your ideal outcome for this meeting/conversation?
- Have you got all the facts?
- What positive feedback can you start with?
- What is the constructive feedback? What are you unhappy with? What specifically do you want instead?
- What positive feedback can you finish with?

When giving feedback, it is important to be as specific as possible. Rather than saying "You did a great job yesterday." it is more constructive to say: "The report you presented at the meeting was well written and clearly demonstrated you have thought through the issues we are facing".

Consider how you might position the "constructive" part of the conversation. Avoid accusing the other person of doing, or not doing, something – just stick to the facts. Focus on the behaviour and the effects, not the individual person, otherwise your feedback may be perceived as an assault on their character.

Even if you are delivering an unwelcome message, you can still maintain rapport. You can do this by matching and mirroring body language, maintaining eye contact, and matching tone, pitch and tempo as we have already discussed in **Chapter Six – Managing Relationships**.

Remember to conduct the conversation from a position of respect, being non-judgemental, and showing genuine curiosity. Take time to listen - you have two ears and one mouth for a reason.

4. PROBLEM-SOLVING

Problems are an everyday occurrence, so I am making the assumption that you will already have had ample experience in solving them. You will have an idea of what works and what does not, therefore this section of the chapter will be a reminder of best practise.

Whatever the problem is, no matter how large or small, the first step is to assess the facts. What information do you already have, who is involved, what has happened, what should have happened, and what do you want to have happen? Gather information from each of those involved, ensure that you listen with respect, suspending judgement and putting personal opinions to one side. Listen carefully to what is being said, and reflect back to confirm that you have understood the facts.

When you look at a problem objectively you will remove any emotion, simply state the facts as you see and hear them. It will help you to remove your personal emotions, your beliefs and your opinions about the other parties are involved. If there is someone involved who you have a low opinion of, beware as this may impact on how you treat them in connection with the situation.

Exercise 8.4 - Problem-Solving Questions

Here are some more questions to help you.
Consider a problem you are currently dealing with, and record the answers to the following questions. Alternatively, ask someone to pose the questions to you and for them to record your response:

1. What is the issue?
2. What are the facts?
3. How is this causing a problem?
4. Who is affected by this problem?
5. What happens if the problem is not resolved?
6. Why do we need to resolve this?
7. Who will benefit?
8. What has already been done to resolve the issue?
9. How has this kind of problem been successfully dealt with before?
10. Consider the issue and ask 'What is important to me (the leader), the team and the organisation in the context of this issue?
11. What are the logical and rational options?
12. How do you feel about these possible solutions?
13. How will these options affect others in the team/ organisation?

Once you have considered a list of possible solutions, select the three most popular or appropriate, and imagine the consequences of each.

What might the repercussions be? Can these be dealt with? What is your next step?

Using a coaching style

Do you find that members of your team and other colleagues tend to come to you with their problems, for both work and non-work issues? A natural inclination is to help the other person and to help them find a solution because we are, after all, 'solution-seeking beings'. As an experienced individual with your life and work experience it will be tempting, and usually far easier, to make suggestions based on the information provided, or to simply tell the person what **you** think they should do. It is quick and the job gets done. That is great, but if you always dish out the answer, the downside is that your colleagues will keep on coming to you with their problems, because they will assume you have the answer.

As a strong leader, you know that you need to develop your team members, to help them learn new tools and techniques. You want to empower and motivate them, but if you are holding onto the information that provides the answer to their problems, and they rely on you for solutions, they are not learning. They are not making decisions or learning to think for themselves.

Maximise your impact as an effective leader by encouraging your team to take on more responsibilities, and give them confidence to make their own decisions. The result will be a more motivated, empowered and self-sufficient workforce, which will free you up to work on the bigger issues.

Leading with a coaching style helps team members to think through the issue at hand and take responsibility for finding their own solutions. Otherwise, when you make a suggestion that does not work, it will be your fault. When a team member starts to talk about a problem and you ask some probing questions, you are facilitating their thinking and raising their self awareness. When they come up with their own solution, then they are more likely to follow through on the action they have decided to take. Coaching helps individuals to process their thoughts through articulating what they are thinking, and helps them to find solutions that will work for them personally.

The GROW Model

Here is one of the widely-used coaching models; the GROW model. This model can be used during a performance review, or it can be used during a five minute conversation, when a team member has come to you with a problem.

G = Goal - what is the issue and what outcome do you want?
R = Reality - establish the current situation, gather the facts, determine what has already been done.
O = Options - explore and brainstorm as many possible solutions or strategies as possible, then refine.
W = Way forward - what are the next steps? Who will action this?

To make the coaching conversation as effective as possible, you must first build rapport with the other person. Your team member will feel comfortable to open up if you can demonstrate that you respect them, that there is mutual trust, and that you are prepared to listen. Some of your team may find it difficult to admit that they are struggling, and will have their own internal dialogue as to what you will think of them - maybe they are uncertain whether they can trust you. When you actively build rapport, they will recognise that you care, and that you are listening at a deeper level, so they will be far more open with their thoughts.

One of the biggest mistakes I see when observing other people coach, is the inability to allow a silence develop for more than a few seconds. If you are asking someone a question that you genuinely want to hear the response to, you must allow the other person time to process the question, and wait for them to formulate and communicate their reply. Here is a small sample of questions for each section of the GROW model. You can try out these the next time someone comes to you for advice.

Top Tips - Coaching Questions

Goal
- What is the issue?
- What do you want to have happen?
- What would you like to achieve from this conversation?
- Why do you want this?

Reality
- Tell me more about 'X'
- Is there anything else?
- What have you done about this already?
- What have you tried that works?
- What's stopping you from finding a solution?
- Use questions 'how', 'what', 'when', 'where' and 'who'.

Options
- What options do you have?
- If you couldn't fail, what might you do?
- What else?
- Which action do you think will work in this situation?

Way Forward
- What is your next step?
- What support do you need?
- What might get in the way?
- How will you overcome this?

Remember to avoid the question 'Why', as this can put the other person onto a defensive footing, particularly when you are at the 'Reality' or 'Options' stage. Asking 'Why' in the goal-setting stage can be useful as this uncovers motivation for achieving the outcome.

Coaching others helps them to clarify their thinking and creates a space to allow them to find alternative solutions. They are more likely to come up with solutions that you might not have thought of yourself.

5. MANAGING CHANGE

To keep growing, and to keep ahead of the competition, organisations are constantly looking for ways to improve, be it more innovative products, better customer service, reduced costs, increased sales, or more effective ways of developing and engaging their staff.

You will recognise the well-known saying, "The only constant in life is change". Change is inevitable, but few people fully embrace it, or find it easy. If change is not handled properly, difficult situations will crop up, which will result in taking up your valuable time to resolve them. When you become more aware of 'change' situations and the possible adverse implications, you can put measures in place to minimise any potential negative impact.

Let us look at the three main changes we encounter in business: people, the organisation itself, and systems.

'People changes' might include new members joining a team, a new boss, new peers, people leaving, or people taking on new roles. This can be the trickiest area to handle, as we each have personal values, beliefs, judgements, fears, expectations, and a minefield of personal emotions to deal with.

'Organisation changes' can involve restructures, office moves, redundancies, takeovers, and mergers. These changes cause uncertainty and fear, and many of these changes then have a knock-on effect, creating more 'people changes' to deal with.

Finally, as organisations grow, they create 'Systems and Processes changes', whereby systems need to be updated, and processes improved. These can be time-consuming, and increase the pressure on already-stretched team members.

Whatever the change is, it will usually impact upon the people in the organisation, and even externally on customers. How you handle the potential repercussions of change will be noted by those around you. To be a strong leader, it is essential to be aware of, and improve, the skills required to manage change.

The Change Curve

It will help you to manage change more effectively if you are familiar with the Change Curve. This model was originally developed in the 1960s by Elisabeth Kübler-Ross to explain the grieving process. The model has been widely adopted by the business world, and is used to help explain how people can be affected by significant changes. It is a useful prediction of how performance can be affected when change is announced and subsequently implemented.

Each person reacts differently to change and their reaction will vary depending on their personality type, knowledge, and past experiences.

The Kubler-Ross change curve

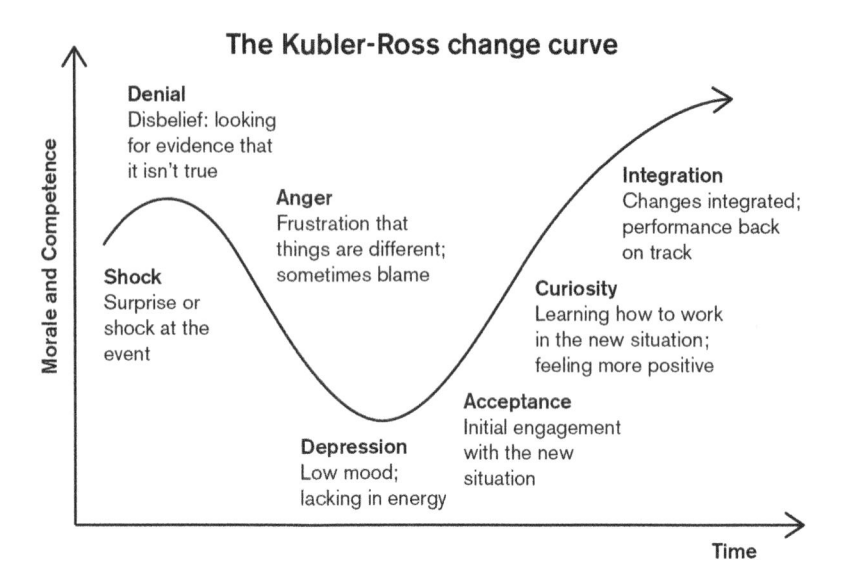

Y-axis: Morale and Competence; X-axis: Time

- **Denial** — Disbelief: looking for evidence that it isn't true
- **Shock** — Surprise or shock at the event
- **Anger** — Frustration that things are different; sometimes blame
- **Depression** — Low mood; lacking in energy
- **Acceptance** — Initial engagement with the new situation
- **Curiosity** — Learning how to work in the new situation; feeling more positive
- **Integration** — Changes integrated; performance back on track

Phase One - The first stage and initial reaction to a significant change is usually shock. Shock can be the result of insufficient information shared regarding the change, which feeds a fear of the unknown, and a fear of making mistakes. This phase may be short-lived, but it will have an impact on performance; people who are usually focused and decisive can become uncertain and look for reassurance.

Once the initial shock has passed, people then move into the second part of the first phase, denial, not really believing that a change is about to happen. They may feel threatened by the change, wanting to remain in a familiar situation, and unable to understand why such a change is necessary.

Phase Two - Once the shock and denial has subsided, anger and even blame can take over. Thoughts of "What a waste of time, I've got better things to do than learn a new piece of software!" can frustrate them, and they will start to blame other people for the situation, principally the IT department whenever software is involved! Common feelings at this stage include frustration, scepticism, and possibly depression. When someone is feeling frustrated, their focus will be on blaming someone or something else, and performance is going to be at its lowest.

Phase Three - The final stage of acceptance and integration comes when people start to accept the change; they can start to see the benefits, and possibly some new opportunities. Performance gets back on track, and there is a healthy curiosity about the change and a desire to be part of it.

When a member of your team is going through change, it is helpful for you to understand where they are on the curve as this will help you respond in the most resourceful way, and recognise what level of support is required.

Managing the stages of the Change Curve

Let us explore the different ways of responding to the three phases just mentioned. During the 'Shock and Denial' phase, communication and openness are essential. As you share more information, this will minimise the fear of the unknown. If you are open about the situation and how **you** are feeling about it, then you can encourage your team to share their concerns. Use your rapport-building and coaching skills, listen with respect, reflect back their concerns using their language, and they will feel as if you understand them. Reassure them as much as possible, and support those who are struggling most. The more effective you are at handling this stage, the easier the following stages will be to handle.

When the 'Anger' stage is apparent, once again you need to be open with your communication ensuring that you are available to answer any questions, and to reassure those affected that other people will be experiencing the same emotions. By encouraging people to share their feelings, and to name them, this will help to soften and diffuse these feelings.

At the final phase of 'Acceptance and Integration', help others to focus on the future and to highlight the progress that is being made. Keep the lines of communication open, encourage feedback, and explore how you can include team members in being a positive part of the change.

Although we have discussed the phases sequentially, it is not unusual for people to experience different feelings at different times, and at different rates. Be aware of this, and the potential for emotional outbursts which could lead to difficult situations. Keep communicating and listening, so you can support your team while minimising a drop in performance.

Handling difficult situations is a small but crucial part of your role. How you manage these situations will have a big impact on how you are perceived by those around you.

Summary

1. Mentally rehearse the ideal scenario of how you want an event to play out.
2. Choosing the right time and location is an important factor when you are planning to instigate or conduct a difficult conversation, particularly if this is within your control.
3. To manage a difficult conversation effectively, and to get the result you want, ensure that you have a good rapport with the other party at all times.
4. Feedback avoidance can be as damaging as avoiding conflict.
5. Encourage your team to take on more responsibilities, and give them confidence to make their own decisions.

6. Practise using the coaching questions when a team member asks for your help.
7. If change is not handled properly then difficult situations are bound to crop up, and will result in a loss of your valuable time to resolve them.

CHAPTER NINE

Managing Time

"Time is at once the most valuable and the most perishable of all our possessions."

John Randolph

Time management is a frequently discussed issue in coaching sessions. There never seems to be enough time to do everything - is this because there are just too many things to do? Are we truly realistic in our expectations of what can be achieved? In our busy schedules, do we factor in enough time for interruptions, phone calls, endless e-mails, or unexpected visitors?

Time management is an extensive topic (there are countless books dedicated to it), but we have room for just one chapter here, so I am going to focus on the main factors which impact upon your time. Remember, it is not time that we need to manage, but how we manage ourselves within the time available.

1. PRIORITISING

Prioritising is the process of making decisions based on what is most important to you. How do you decide what you are going to do first on your daily 'To Do' list? Few people manage to get everything finished. Maybe you are one of the many who stay late to ensure the essentials tasks are completed?

Have you noticed those items on your list that never quite get completed, but carried over to the next day/week/month? What is it that compels you to complete one action and yet push another to one side?

We all have different ways of tackling our 'To Do' lists. These will include factors such as personality style, decision-making process, motivation, capability, and who will ultimately benefit from the completion of the task.

What drives you to take action is your motivation, and behind this motivation are all the unconscious factors listed above – and probably a few more. The thing is, you will not fully understand what is preventing you from getting on with a task, until you pause and think about what really is stopping you.

Take out your journal and complete the following exercise to uncover how your unconscious mind is prioritising the list for you.

Exercise 9.1 - Prioritising your 'To Do' List

Look at your current To Do list – just take the top 5 items for now and for each item:
1. Rate on a scale of 1 – 10 how important this task is (10 being very important).
2. How many minutes/hours will the task take?
3. Who will benefit from this task being completed?
4. Who will give you recognition for completing the task?
5. Rate on a scale of 1-10 whether you will enjoy completing the task (10 being high).

How do you decide which task to complete first? Is it the easiest, the quickest, the one you will enjoy doing the most, or the one which will impress your boss? Does your method help you to get through a large volume of tasks quickly, therefore providing a sense of achievement, or does it provide you with external recognition?

When you can see that certain tasks are not getting done, what will motivate you to get them done? What can you say to yourself that will compel you to take action on an item that you do not enjoy doing, yet know needs to be done? Consider these responses and jot them down in your journal.

The five D's

Most people's task lists are long and varied. In my experience, far too much time is wasted reviewing lists and deciding what to do first, which results in the important tasks not getting done. Try this exercise to sort out your 'To Do' lists and apply the five D's.

Exercise 9.2 - The Five D's

Review your list and write one of the following words against each item
- Do
- Delegate
- Diarise
- Defer
- Dump

Do it – if a task will take less than 5 minutes, just do it.
Delegate it – to someone else who is just as capable – we talk more about this shortly.
Diarise it – this will be for tasks that take 30 minutes to 2 hours, you must allocate time in your diary to ensure the task is completed, otherwise you will keep putting it off.
Defer it – does the item need to be done this week? If not, move it to a Long Term Goals document, and pull it down at the appropriate time.
Dump it – for items that are just not getting done! Review the task, assess the importance of the task, and either use one of the other D's or dump it!

2. GOAL SETTING

Goal setting is probably the most fundamental part of time management, and yet this can easily be overlooked. If you are not clear on what you want to achieve, and do not have an outline of the steps needed to get there, how can you monitor your progress and ensure that you are moving in the right direction? As Stephen Covey says in ***The 7 Habits of Highly Effective People***, *"It's incredibly easy to get caught up in an activity trap, in the busyness of life, to work harder and harder at climbing the ladder of success, only to discover it's leaning against the wrong wall."*

In Chapter Four you started to get clarity around your long-term vision, and began to break it down into achievable milestones. This gave you a plan, or a schedule to work towards, to ensure that you take action on a regular basis to propel you forwards.

Check that you have tasks on your daily 'To Do' list that will ensure you reach your milestones, and ultimately your long-term goals. Of course you have your day-to-day responsibilities, but are you completing tasks on your 'Not Urgent, but Important' list each day?

Set up and populate a working 'Long-Term Goals' document. Decide which of your goals you consider to be long-term, perhaps to be achieved in 12 or 24 months? These are the goals that will move you closer to your vision. Break these long-term goals down into 'Milestones'; these will be short-term goals for the month or quarter, to ensure your long-term goals remain on track.

Re-visit the milestones on a regular basis (weekly or monthly), transferring additional smaller tasks to your Daily or Weekly 'To Do' list to ensure that each stage of the milestone is completed on time. I know that this is easier said than done, but it is a good start, and a good habit to get into.

Once you have completed a difficult task, or achieved a milestone, stop to celebrate your achievement, with your team or those who were involved, before rushing onto the next one. You may find it encouraging to record your achievements, so that you can reflect on, and acknowledge progress with your team.

3. PROCRASTINATION

Taking action is the only way to get things done. It might sound obvious, but we all have items on our list that need to be completed, and yet they get ignored or relegated because there are always other more pressing tasks demanding attention.

Procrastination & disorganisation are integrally linked. Once you have started to prioritise, and work through your 'To Do' list, procrastination will become less of an issue. There will be other factors preventing you from getting started on a task; the project is so big you do not know where to start, the project is not interesting enough, the deadline is so far away, the fear of failure, or maybe you simply do not like doing the task.

Throughout years of coaching team leaders, I have noticed that people tend to put off important tasks because they are too overwhelming, complex, or time-consuming to handle.

Top Tips - Tackle Procrastination

Here are some tips to get you started. Find one of those important, but not urgent, tasks on your list.
1. Pick a small task related to the main project and start it.
2. Follow this task with another small, easy and instant task.
3. With this process you are literally chipping away at the

big task. Soon you will have taken a big chunk out of the project, and as you become more and more involved, it all becomes much easier.
4. Use the same technique for the unpleasant tasks – do small five minute tasks then do something else.

An excellent book to help you tackle procrastination is ***Eat that Frog*** by Brian Tracy.

4. PERFECTIONISM

Another reason for not getting things done, is waiting until you have everything 'just right' before you feel you can start. Maybe you keep going over a document, fine-tuning it, adding a bit here, changing something there, and delaying sending it out for fear that it is not 'perfect'. Some people feel that they have to give more than 100% on everything they do, particularly at the beginning of a new role. Striving for perfection, whether it is producing the perfect proposal or preparing the perfect presentation, can take up enormous amounts of time, and often it is unnecessary.

If you have an embedded need to be 'perfect', and are forever striving to be seen as such, it can have a detrimental effect. Instead of maximising your impact, you will be reducing it.

Striving for perfection will serve you well to a degree, in that it will help you to achieve high standards and you will produce excellent work, but remember that true perfection is an unattainable illusion.

The term 'Perfectionism' refers to a set of self-defeating thoughts and behaviours, aimed at reaching excessively high and unrealistic goals. A question I often ask clients who recognise this trait in themselves is: "When did you decide to be a perfectionist?" Of course most people do not consciously decide to be so; it tends to stem from a time in their early years when they enjoyed recognition for their achievements, and now they are still searching for more of that praise.

Approval from others

If you are a perfectionist, it is possible you learned early in life that other people valued you on the basis of how much you achieved. As a result, you may have become dependent upon other people's approval, which can leave you overly sensitive to external opinions and criticism. In attempting to protect yourself from such criticism, you have decided that striving for perfection is your only defence.

This is another large and complex topic, and there are varying degrees of perfectionism. It can take a while to uncover where your beliefs about perfection derive from, requiring a qualified coach or therapist.

In the meantime, here are some ideas to consider which will help you to relax your need for perfectionism

Top Tips - Manage Perfectionism

1. Set goals based on your own needs, rather than perceived expectations of others.
2. Instead of aiming for 100% perfection, aim for 80% to reduce the pressure on yourself.
3. What would 80% look/feel or sound like?
4. Consider the result, and rather than asking yourself if it is perfect, ask 'Is it good enough'?

5. Confront the fears that may be behind your perfectionism by asking yourself, "What am I afraid of?", or "What is the worst thing that could happen?"

When you decide to let go of being a perfectionist, it will free up more time to spend doing what is really important to you.

5. INTERRUPTIONS

If all you had to do each day was to work through your 'To Do' list, there would be relatively few books and articles on the subject of time management. However, we all know that life is not like that, with endless interruptions and distractions for us to deal with throughout the day.

Some people are more prone to interruptions than others, and that is because these people actually welcome distractions. If your personality style is that of somebody who enjoys variety, spontaneity and novelty, then you will welcome any distraction that captures your attention. Once you are aware of this tendency, you can set up the tasks on your list to be done in short bursts of time, and you can move between tasks, chipping away at each one, giving you the variety that stimulates you. Just make sure that you fully complete sufficient tasks each day.

If you are a person who likes structure and routine, then you will find it easier to focus on the task in hand, and work at it until it is complete.

Interruptions and distractions can rule your life if you let them. When you are in a senior role, everybody wants a piece of your time; the telephone rings, urgent e-mails arrive, people pop in, extra tasks emerge, and meetings overrun. Before you know it, you are only halfway through your 'To Do' list, and you must leave for the day.

Some interruptions appear so urgent that your own plans are relegated to the bottom of the list. To regain control, you will need to minimise the interruptions that are taking you away from your core tasks.

A good place to start is to keep a time diary and record what, and who, are your interruptions. Apart from the usual suspects – e-mail, telephone, clients, prospects, and colleagues – what else is interrupting you from doing what you need to do? Here are some suggestions to manage the distractions and interruptions that can be potentially wasting your time.

Telephone

For many leaders I have noticed that telephone interruptions are now less of a problem than they used to be, because e-mails and text have taken their place. However, there are still telephone calls that cause interruptions and take away valuable time.

If phone calls are draining minutes, or hours, from your day, try these ideas:

Top Tips - Minimise Telephone Interruptions

1. If you have blocked out time to work on a task that needs your full concentration, divert your phone or use a 'call handler' to manage incoming calls.
2. Ask people if you can call them back at an allotted time.
3. Get into the habit of scheduling a specific time for calls,

i.e. early in the day. Take the initiative to contact the other party – then you can call them at your convenience.
4. Practise the art of 'short' phone calls. When receiving a call, rather than asking "How are you?" ask "What can I do for you?" Get to the point quickly, be clear & concise. Keep it short, yet friendly, and make a graceful exit.
5. Before making a call, decide what you want from the call, plan your conversation, listen and take notes to save any confusion.

E-mail

E-mail is a wonderfully unobtrusive way of communicating, and yet many people are totally overwhelmed by the volume of e-mails in their inboxes. One client was struggling with over 50,000 e-mails in his inbox, with an extra 500 being added daily. If you are not in control of your inbox, then how can you keep up to date, and communicate effectively?

It is time to take back control of your inbox; get organised and treat your inbox as you used to treat your 'In-tray'. Consider e-mails as replacement letters or memos, and therefore deal with them in a similar fashion.

It will take a small investment of time to get the foundations in place, but once done, you will free up much more time to work on the important tasks.

Top Tips - Manage your Inbox

- Unsubscribe from unnecessary mailing lists.
- Are you being copied in on e-mails unnecessarily? Ask to be removed from distribution lists if appropriate.
- If you get too many jokes/chain letters, ask friends to remove you from their lists.
- Set up Spam filters. Set up your inbox software to organise incoming mail, i.e. if you receive newsletters that you do not want to read immediately, these can go straight into your 'Newsletter' folder, to be read at a later date.
- Set up folders for different projects you are working on.
- Set a regular time to check incoming e-mail & when to respond.
- Turn off the automatic alert so that you are not distracted.
- Set up folders on your computer and allocate to the following:
    - Deal with today - set a time to deal with them.
    - Deal with this week.
    - Deal with this month - or whatever works for you.
- Remember, e-mails are pieces of correspondence and they need filing in order, and in places where you can easily locate them if needed.
- Save attachments into Word documents if you really need to keep them, and file appropriately. This will free up space in your inbox.
- Where appropriate, ask your IT department for help.

When you get into the habit of managing your inbox, you will be creating more time to focus on the important strategic tasks.

Interruptions Record

If you suffer from interruptions other than e-mail & telephone, keep a log of your 'Time Stealers'. If these interruptions are valid, then you will need to build them into your schedule, if not, you will need to find a way to block them out. Even if interruptions are part and parcel of your job, and you need to 'be available' to your team, you can still allocate times when it is okay to be interrupted, and times when you should be left alone, unless there is an emergency.

Whilst you will want to stick to your schedule whenever possible, do not become excessively rigid. Deal with emergencies that need to be dealt with and take relevant opportunities that come up.

The biggest culprits for distractions and time stealing, can be your own internal dialogue and attention span. If you are working on a large project, build in regular coffee/tea breaks, so that after ten minutes you will be fresh and ready to return to work. If you sense your mind is wandering and looking for distraction (e.g. re-organising your Contacts list), I find that having a big yellow 'sticky' on my screen "ARE YOU INVENTING THINGS TO DO?" is a useful reminder to get me back on track.

6. DELEGATION

When you reviewed your 'To Do' list, did you see tasks on it that somebody else could do just as easily? Are you guilty of holding onto tasks because it is quicker to do so, rather than showing somebody else how to do it? If you are holding onto tasks which you could be delegating, then you are taking up valuable time that you could be using to greater impact on more productive leadership tasks.

Exercise 9.3 - Delegation Barriers

Take out your journal and consider: "What is stopping me from delegating?"

Here are some of the common 'reasons' I hear:
- It's quicker to do it myself.
- There's no-one else to delegate to.
- Everyone else is busy.
- No-one will do it properly.
- I don't have time to show someone else how to do it.
- It only takes five minutes.

Which of these are fact, and which are beliefs?

Let us look at some of those beliefs.

- *It's quicker to do it myself.*

Note down which tasks you think you could delegate, estimate roughly how long you think each task should take, then total up the expected time. In a month, how many hours could you be freeing up to do something more productive? And how long would it take you to show someone else to do these tasks? Probably a small fraction of the time it would free up for you.

- *Everyone else is busy.*

People around you will look busy; we can all fill the time we have available when at work. Check just how busy your team really are, and ask who is willing to take on some extra tasks. You might be surprised with the response.

- *No-one will do it properly.*

This links back to the section on perfectionism, you may have exceptionally high standards and want the job done properly. But when you hold on to tasks that others could be doing, you are holding your team back from growing and developing. By delegating and teaching your team members how to do some of your tasks, you are empowering and motivating them. They want to learn new things and to be given responsibilities, and they will appreciate you putting your trust in them. If you have unsuccessfully delegated a task in the past, and it was not done efficiently, then you need to examine your communication method. When you are tied up with other more pressing tasks, and if you have taken the time to delegate, then you will have others willing to step in and help you out.

- *I don't have time to show someone else to do it.*

This is the same excuse as "It's quicker to do it myself." Remember that taking ten minutes to explain a task, will save you multiples of that time in the future. Also, when you delegate such a task, it can empower the other person, having been chosen by you to undertake something on your behalf.

- *It only takes five minutes.*

All those small tasks that only take five minutes, can add up into hours. If it really is a quick and easy task which only takes five or ten minutes, pass it on to someone else to do.

When you delegate a task, ensure that you communicate clearly what needs to be done, and give the other person the responsibility of reporting back with progress. Check that they have completed the task to your standard, and give appropriate feedback. When you delegate a task, this does not mean that you are abdicating responsibility, you must still continue to oversee that the tasks are being completed correctly.

7. MEETINGS

As a leader you will be required to attend a variety of meetings, and for many people, these take up a large percentage of available time. Managers and directors often tell me of their frustration with meetings; either they start late, overrun, or result in no agreed actions being followed through. Also, far too often, their presence turns out to be completely unnecessary.

How much of your valuable time is being taken up by poorly-organised, or poorly-led meetings, and what can you do about it?

Daniel

Daniel was a newly-appointed Marketing Manager, having been promoted from within the same organisation. He was now attending boardroom meetings with people to whom he used to report. He was surprised at the poor organisation of the meetings, particularly as they were chaired by his boss, who was the Marketing Director. He was becoming increasingly frustrated by the time wasted at the beginning of each meeting, which was taken up reviewing unfinished actions from previous meetings. Furthermore, the meetings rarely started on time, and never finished on time, which was impacting his already-busy schedule.

As a newcomer, Daniel didn't feel as if he had the authority to comment on, or improve, the running of the meetings. We addressed this issue in one of Daniel's coaching sessions, because the time wasted was impacting upon his schedule, resulting in him having to work late to keep on top of his tasks. Daniel realised that he needed to discuss the situation with his boss, Franco, the Marketing Director.

Daniel was already having weekly meetings with Franco, to share his progress and discuss ongoing issues, so this was the ideal forum to air his concerns. Daniel clarified in advance what he wanted to achieve from the meeting, and rehearsed in his mind how the conversation would play out. He had already prepared some bullet points, detailing how the meetings were impacting upon his other responsibilities, and suggesting ways to improve the time-keeping. He knew that he had to be tactful in how he presented the information, particularly as Franco was the reason for the ineffective meetings!

Daniel used his rapport-building skills and was careful to keep his comments objective, rather than making it a personal attack on Franco. Daniel knew that Franco liked logic and rationale, so he put forward his case in those terms. He also knew that he needed to feel confident, assertive, and in control, so we set an anchor for Daniel to trigger when he needed it.

Franco was impressed with Daniel's honesty, and agreed to make some significant changes to how the meetings were run, ensuring they started on time, whether or not everyone was present. He introduced a timed agenda, and ensured the meetings finished promptly. Just a few changes to how the meeting was organised and conducted, freed up time not just for Daniel, but also for the other meeting attendees.

8. JUST SAY 'NO'

Your time at work will be taken up with tasks relating to your role, and then there will be other jobs that you have agreed to undertake, ones which might not necessarily be in your job description. Just as you delegate, so there will be others who delegate to you. If you are new to your role, or to the organisation, you will want to make a good impression, and to be seen as willing, so naturally you will be happy to help others and to agree to their requests. This is fine, so long as the tasks are relevant and you have time to complete them. When I work with overwhelmed leaders, the problem has often developed because they have found it difficult to refuse requests, for fear of appearing unhelpful.

How many requests have you agreed to recently, that are causing you to fall behind in your own work? How many of these requests would you like to have declined, but felt you could not? And importantly, what stopped you from saying 'no' at the time?

Exercise 9.4 - Learning to Say NO

Consider the questions you need to ask yourself, to help assess whether you agree to a request, and record your thoughts in your journal.

They might include questions such as:
- Who will benefit from me taking on this request (task/meeting)?
- How long will it take?
- How will it impact on my other responsibilities?
- Is this more important that my current priorities?
- What will happen if I don't accept the request?

What other questions will help you to make the decision? Or is there just one question that will do the trick?
Consider these questions before you accept a request, and if necessary let the other person know that you need to consider your response before making a final decision.

If you agree to every request made of you, those around you may see you as a dumping ground, and will pass on their unwanted tasks and meetings to you. If you are busy doing other people's jobs then you will not have time to achieve the results expected of you, and your team. You will end up overworked, overwhelmed, and unable to function efficiently. You are a role model to your team, so you need to practise what you preach.

A useful book here is ***The One Minute Manager meets the Monkey*** by Ken Blanchard, William Oncken and Hal Burrows.

9. GETTING ORGANISED

Do you spend too much time trying to find documents, e-mails, or customer information that has not been filed away? Maybe you have piles of papers on your desk to ensure that all information is close to hand, so that you can dip in and out of projects should you need to? Look critically at your office/desk, and honestly ask yourself whether it is as organised as it could be?

You might like to have everything to hand, but how much time are you wasting looking bits of paper? If your desk is cluttered, then your mind will be cluttered. Time is wasted when you are disorganised, or unstructured in your approach to getting jobs done.

It is worth investing the time to put good systems in place. Set up a filing system so that you can find documents easily; this applies to your inbox as well as your physical documents. If you do not have the time to do so yourself, ask an organised member of your team, or someone who has the time and the skills to do it.

Once you have such a system set up, use it! Decide when is the best time for you to file away information, either at regular intervals during the day, or last thing in the evening before you go home, so that everything is in order when you return the next day. If you are not sure what kind of system will work for you, find some role models and find out what they do.

You will be surprised at how much more focused and organised you are, and how much time it will free up for you to do the important tasks.

10. MOTIVATION

Your mindset, and how you feel, will both have a big impact on what you can get done. If you are feeling stressed, tired, or emotional, your motivation levels will be lower than usual and you will not be in the mood for taking action. To get things done, you need energy and motivation. When you are feeing low and de-motivated, how do you pick yourself up and get energised again?

If you are feeling tired and cannot focus, then sometimes you need to give yourself permission to put a particular task to one side, and to use your time instead doing something which needs to be done, but which does not require full concentration. At least you are moving things off your 'To Do' list. If you need to take a break, take one. Go for a walk, get some fresh air, and then find a strategy to help you get motivated once again.

When you recognise that you are feeling stressed, or lacking in confidence, stop, and notice what thoughts are going through your mind at the time. Perhaps you are mulling over negative thoughts such as: "I just can't be bothered today", "What's the point?" or "There's so much to do, I don't know where to start."

Any of these negative thoughts will send a message to your unconscious mind, transmitting feelings of lethargy. Your unconscious mind will start looking for some kind of easy distraction, such as getting a drink, checking e-mails, or planning your next weekend away. To counteract this, decide what kind of thoughts would be more helpful and energise you to take action.

Exercise 9.5 - Motivation Magic

If you are not feeling motivated to tackle what needs to be done, assess where your motivation level is now (on a scale of 1 – 10).

Let us assume you have rated it to be a level 5.
- If you woke up tomorrow morning, and it had magically increased overnight to become a 7, how would you know?
- What would you be doing?
- If I could see you, what would I see you doing differently?
- Write out a description of what you are doing now that you are more motivated, how are you walking, talking, who are you talking to, what is different?
- What are you thinking about?
- Keep building on this picture and then write down as many descriptive words as you can to explain how it feels when you are feeling more motivated.
- When you read back what you have written, if you could just do one thing that would give you that feeling of motivation, and spur you to take action, what would it be?
- Build a list of activities and strategies that get you into a motivated mindset, and refer to this when you need a boost.

Record your notes in your journal.

Twenty Four Hours

Managing time is not difficult. We all have twenty four hours in the day. It is remembering that you can choose what you do with the time available. You can agree to take on other people's tasks, accept that you do not mind fumbling around for lost information, or spend too much time on phone calls. Alternatively, you can chose to be more assertive, more organised, and let go of some of your old beliefs about perfection. Make your choices wisely.

Summary

1. It is not time that we need to manage, it is how we manage ourselves within the time available.
2. Start with the end in mind, by clarifying what you want to achieve.
3. Break a big project into small steps and allocate time in your diary to get one of the steps done. Review the **Top Tips for Procrastination**.
4. True perfection is an illusion that is unattainable.
5. To regain control you will need to minimise the interruptions that are taking you away from your core tasks. Make sure you complete your Interruptions Log.
6. Take back control of your inbox, get organised and treat your inbox as you would treat your 'in tray'.
7. When you delegate a task, ensure that you communicate clearly what needs to be done, and give the other person the responsibility of reporting back with progress.
8. Clear the clutter!

CHAPTER TEN
Getting a Balance

"Don't confuse having a career with having a life."

Hillary Rodham Clinton

Many new leaders tend to adopt a workaholic culture once they start to climb the career ladder. Some of my clients leave home at 6am, and if they are lucky, return back around 8pm, arriving just in time to kiss their children goodnight. Many embark on coaching programmes feeling overwhelmed, having to take work home with them in the evenings, answering e-mails at weekends, and frequently taking a laptop on holiday in order to catch up in the early hours before the family wakes up.

Does this sound familiar? It seems to be acceptable nowadays to work like this, forever playing catch-up, spending personal time preparing for early morning meetings, or leaving home on a Sunday to arrive at a conference venue the night before an early start.

The Mayonnaise Jar and The Glass of Wine

When things in your life seem almost too much to handle, when 24 hours in a day are not enough, remember the mayonnaise jar and the glass of wine.

One morning a professor of philosophy stood in front of his class and wordlessly began to fill a very large and empty mayonnaise jar with golf balls. He then asked the students if the jar was full. They agreed that it was. The professor picked up a box of tiny pebbles and tipped them into the jar.

He shook the jar lightly allowing the pebbles to roll into the open areas between the golf balls before asking the students if the jar was full. They agreed it was.

Next the professor poured a box of sand into the jar filling up all the remaining space and once more asked his class if the jar was full.

The students responded with a unanimous "yes." The professor then produced a glass of wine from under the table and poured the entire contents into the jar, the students laughed.

"Now," said the professor, as the laughter subsided, "I want you to recognise that this jar represents your life. The 'golf balls' are the important things; your family, your children, your health, your friends and your passions.

In other words, all those things that if everything else was lost and if only they remained your life would still be full. The 'pebbles' are the other things that matter like your job, your house, your car, holidays, etc. The sand is everything else, all the small stuff. Now if you put the sand into the jar first," he continued, "there is no room for the 'pebbles' or the 'golf balls'.

The same goes for life. If you spend all your time and energy on the small stuff, you will never have room for the things that are truly important to you.

So pay attention to the things that are critical to your happiness, play with your children, take care of your health, make time for your friends and go out to dinner with your partner because there will always be time to clean the house and fix the car. Set your priorities and take care of the 'golf balls' first for they are the things that really matter, all the rest is just sand."

One of the students raised her hand and asked, "What does the wine represent?" The professor smiled, "I'm glad you asked. I was also showing you that no matter how full your life may seem there's always room for a glass of wine with a friend."

       Author thought to be Mary Lynn Plaisance

1. WORK-LIFE BALANCE

Who is setting the standards and expectations that you should be at your desk an hour before everyone else, but should also be the last to leave? Is it written into your contract that you must respond to e-mails outside work hours, to be available 24/7? If you are a doctor, work shifts, or have an IT support role, you may be required to be 'on call', but that is a small proportion of the working population. Many people work extra hours simply to keep on top of things.

As a leader, you are setting the standards for your team, so if you arrive at the office at 7am and leave at 7pm, your team may feel under pressure to do the same, and may feel guilty if they go home before you.

What impact are these unspoken demands and self-imposed standards having on your health and your relationships at home? Are you making time for the 'golf balls' in your life (your family, health, relationships), or are you spending too much time on the 'pebbles' and filling your life with sand?

How much longer can you continue working at this level before you start to burnout? If you are working excessively long hours on a regular basis, complete the following exercise to start exploring the consequences.

> **Exercise 10.1 - The Consequences**
>
> Make a list here, or in your journal, of the benefits of working long hours:
> _____
> _____

_____
_____

Now consider the negative impact that working long hours are having on you personally, and on those you care about:

_____
_____
_____
_____

- Step into the shoes of your partner, one of your children or a good friend, what do they think the impact is when you work such long hours?
- How does it affect you, them and your relationship?
- When you are in the shoes of your best friend, partner, son/daughter, based on the answers above, what advice would they want to give you?

Now consider what you can, and would like to, change. What is within your control? Note your thoughts in your journal.

Often, the reason for working long hours, is simply because you have too much to do. If this is the case, then I suggest you revisit the previous chapter, and start analysing what, or who, is stealing your time. Consider which areas you need to address to free up your time, whether it is prioritising, perfectionism, or delegation. If you fail to address your work/life balance and focus on your own wellbeing, you may end up without a family to go home to, and will berate yourself for working so hard.

It is time to challenge the long working hours culture, and ensure that the time you spend at work is used effectively and efficiently to obtain results. Now is a good time to find that seemingly elusive work-life balance.

When your work-life balance is out of kilter, you will know about it. You may feel constantly tired, disinterested in life, or have a niggling sense of something missing. It could just take one small thing to trigger an emotional outburst, and you may find it more difficult to bounce back when things do not go according to plan.

Jane

I worked with a client recently who was feeling trapped on her own self-imposed treadmill. For years she had worked hard, spending long days in the office, travelling extensively, and she had managed to climb the corporate ladder. Because status and achievement were important to her in her twenties, she had made the decision to sacrifice her personal life, and pushed away her natural desire to settle down and start a family. The result was financial independence and stability, giving her a beautiful house by the river, the car of her dreams, and a wardrobe full of designer outfits.

Working long hours, and taking conference calls late into the evenings had taken their toll on Jane's friendships, and after several failed relationships, she awoke one morning to realise that her weekends were empty and she had few interests or friends outside of her working life.

Just as we started working together, Jane was made redundant. Losing her job took away her identity and her daily routine. Now there was much more work to be done with Jane than her initial goal to re-establish a social life. She had mistaken her job for a 'golf ball', when in fact it was just a 'pebble'. Yes, it was important, but it didn't leave any room for the golf balls.

When you spend most of your waking hours working, and due to circumstances outside of your control, your role is taken away from you, not only will there be a gaping hole in your career path, but it will highlight how empty the rest of your life is.

Try the following exercise to see how balanced your life is right now.

Exercise 10.2 - The Balanced Wheel

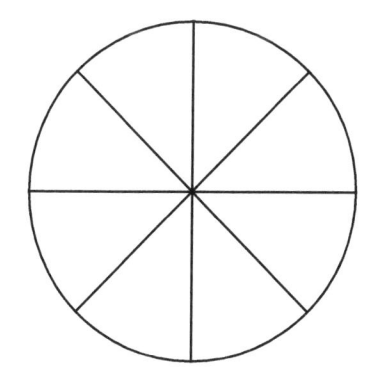

Label each section of the wheel with some of the following headings/areas. Select the areas that are most important to you, or add an area that you feel is missing from the list below.
- Work/Career
- Health
- Fitness
- Finances
- Life partner
- Family
- Social Life
- Interests/hobbies
- House and home

1. Once you have labelled each section, consider how satisfied you are with that element of your life and rate each one on a scale of 1 – 10 (10 being very satisfied).

2. Now consider which of these areas is most important to you. Prioritise your list and ask yourself how much time you are actually committing to this area of your life. For example, if family is your top priority, how much quality time are you spending with your family? If health is important to you, how much time do you spend looking after your health? For many clients, this is a wake-up call, and highlights which areas of their lives are being starved of attention. When you are living an unbalanced life, you will feel flat, unfulfilled, and de-motivated.

3. Select an area that you would like to improve. If you could improve this area by just 2 notches (so if it is 5/10 and you want it to be 7/10) what would you be doing differently?

4. Paint a picture in your mind's eye that demonstrates that you have improved this area. Make it a realistic picture that shows you what you would be doing, and who you would be doing it with. Jot down one or two actions that you can take this week to make some improvements in this area.

2. PERSONAL RELATIONSHIPS

Our lives revolve around relationships with others. Your partner, children, family and friends, are your 'golf balls'. It is up to you how you relate to them and how fulfilling, or draining, the relationships are.

Why do we need to address personal and social relationships in a book about soft skills for strong leaders? Well, the quality of your relationships, both inside and outside of work, will impact on how you feel about yourself, which will in turn affect your behaviour, and how you deal with day-to-day work issues.

Mentally absent

Can you remember the last time you had a disagreement with a friend, partner, or family member? Did you switch off thinking about it as soon as you arrived at work, or did it impact your mood for the rest of the day? Did you spend time re-living the conversation in your mind, planning how you could make amends, or how you could take revenge? You may be physically present at your desk, but mentally absent, if something from your private life is playing on your mind. We have already covered topics such as 'Managing your Mindset' and 'Emotions' - refer back to these chapters if you have a habit of daydreaming, or bringing personal issues to work.

Drains and radiators

We all have human drains and radiators in our lives, both in and outside of work. Drains are the negative people, who focus on all the things going wrong around them, and who are only too happy to point out what they disapprove about you and your life. After having spent time with them, you feel exhausted and sucked dry.

Radiators are people you warm to, who generate energy and warmth, and to whom you are naturally drawn. The radiators in your life make you feel good about yourself, and about life. When you spend time with them, you are filled with motivation and enthusiasm. Surround yourself with radiators and reduce the time you spend with drains, and you will find that you have more energy at home, and at work. It is worth noting that people who are more extroverted derive their energy from being around other people. Introverts will need to limit the time they spend with large groups, and particularly exuberant people, as they can drain them of energy.

Support network

Developing healthy relationships with friends and family, will provide you with support when needed, and will enable you to give it back in return, when required. Spending time with people who you like, and with whom you have similar interests with, is fun, and helps you to relax and switch off when you are outside work. Relationships do not always develop naturally, they need to be nurtured, and if you neglect them they can wither and die. So, how do you nurture your relationships and keep in touch with friends when you are so busy at work Mondays to Fridays, and often at the weekend? Try the following exercise.

Exercise 10.3 - Time for Personal Relationships

In order to improve your relationships, the first step is to decide what you want to achieve. Here are some questions to get started:
1. Assess how satisfied you are with your relationships at the moment. You can take this information from the last exercise.
2. Consider one of your main relationship categories, i.e. partner or friends, and if you were to rate this category at 10/10 (meaning that you are totally satisfied) what would be different?
3. Why is it important to you to improve this relationship?
4. If the rating was 10/10, consider what you would see,

hear and feel that would tell you that you are happy with this relationship.
5. What is getting in the way of achieving this?
6. What can you do to overcome this obstacle?
7. If you could do just one thing this week to move you closer to that vision, what would it be?
8. Is this a step that you can realistically take this week? If not, when?

Record your thoughts in your journal.

As much as you want to spend time with your family and friends, there is a limit to what you can do and how much time you can spare. When you are not at work, it is essential to establish a balance between 'friend/family-time', and 'me-time'. Spending time with others can be uplifting, but spending time alone is equally as important.

3. TIME FOR YOU

Establishing a healthy work-life balance, includes finding time when you can relax and switch off from work. Having outside hobbies and interests is an excellent way of achieving this.

What do you enjoy doing when you are not working, travelling, or doing the domestic chores? Is it something that relaxes you, or exhilarates you? You might not have had the time to think about this before, so spend ten minutes now.

Exercise 10.4 - Relax/Excite/Challenge

1. Imagine that you have been given an extra two days off next week, and you could do anything at all. Without judgement, what would you do? Would you do something to relax, to excite you or challenge you?
2. Make three columns and head each column with the words Relax, Excite, Challenge, then list at least five activities or items under each one.
- For example, under **Relax** you might put: have a scented bath, play music, swim, read, spend time in the garden, cook, walk.
- For **Excite** you might have: Go to the races, skydiving, white water rafting, go to a live concert, explore a new city.
- Under **Challenge** you might have: Cycle from Vietnam to Cambodia, renovate a piece of furniture, raise funds for a charity, climb the Three Peaks. I'm sure you can think of a lot more.
3. Once you have a list under each heading, decide which one you would like to pursue, and do something about it. It might take some organising, but once you have a few things in your diary other than work, you will start to feel more fulfilled and motivated AT work.
4. Cast your eye over your list of suggestions to relax and consider how often in the last six months have you done any of the activities? How would it benefit you if you were to build in time on a daily/weekly basis to relax?

If you have a young and demanding family at home, you might feel that time for relaxation is short, yet it is crucial to find time to recharge your batteries, so that you can give more to others. If you are a parent, you will be used to putting others first and feel that there is no time left for you. However, remember the advice we get when we board an airplane with children; if there should be a drop in cabin pressure and the oxygen masks appear, you must put the oxygen mask on yourself first, and then the child. When you look after yourself first, you will be stronger and more able to look after the other significant people in your life.

Make yourself a priority

How often do you make yourself the priority? You might not always have the luxury of doing this on a day-to-day basis, but if you can build in some time a few times a week, then not only are you in a better place to support others, but you are also respecting yourself and your needs.

Have you had a holiday recently? If you are employed, you will probably take at least an annual holiday, but do you switch off and have a proper break? Or do you take work away with you, so that you can keep up-to-date with what is happening in your absence, and maintain some form of control? Getting a holiday booked in the diary can be an achievement in itself, but for many, the preparation of getting up-to-date before leaving, and then the thought of picking up the pieces again upon returning, can put the dampers on a holiday before even boarding the plane.

Leaders often find going on holiday stressful, as there are seldom others to take their place and make decisions whilst they are away. So how can you prepare for this, and leave the office for two weeks, knowing that you do not have to worry? How can you continue to have a positive impact even when you are not there? Jot down your thoughts in your journal.

If your colleagues know that you respond to e-mails when on holiday, then they will contact you, and expect a response. Let them know that you will not be contactable, delegate someone to make decisions in your absence, and you will have managed their expectations.

4. LOOKING AFTER YOUR BODY

Taking a holiday, finding time to relax, and having interests outside of work will certainly enhance your mental and physical well-being, putting you in a far stronger position to perform your leadership duties than when you are feeling tired and washed out.

Healthy eating

Although we may not be qualified nutritionists, we are sufficiently educated to know that what we put into our bodies, has a physical impact on our performance. Surviving on fast food, sugar-filled cakes, and three course lunches/dinners, will cause you to put on weight and feel sluggish. When you feel overweight and lethargic, your motivation levels drop, and your results will reflect this.

The flip side of this is, if you do not make time to eat properly, or forget to eat breakfast or lunch, you could be losing weight without realising it, depriving yourself of energy and mental alertness.

When you are busy, it is tempting to resort to the quickest and easiest options to satisfy your hunger; this might mean a morning coffee or croissant at the station, lunchtime sandwiches at your desk, and a late evening meal when you get home. Poor eating habits are the result of a lack of planning - if your weight and energy levels are a problem, then you must make a conscious decision to do something about it.

If you are not sure what you need to do to be eating more healthily, and to incorporate this into your lifestyle, find a local, qualified nutritionist who will design a meal plan for you and your circumstances. If you have already started to make some changes to how you spend your time, having read the chapter on time management, then you will have no excuse to find the time to plan your meals in advance. If you are still struggling with low energy levels, find your local Kinesiologist or consult your doctor to explore whether you have any food intolerances.

Great reasons to exercise

Here are some great reasons for making time in your busy schedule to get your heart rate pumping.

1. Exercise improves your mood - it stimulates various chemicals in your brain that gives you an emotional uplift and it relaxes you too. When you exercise regularly, you feel better about yourself, and your appearance.
2. Exercising burns calories - You do not need to work out for hours each day; just a half-hour walk at lunchtime, or taking the stairs instead of the lift can make a big difference.
3. Exercise gives you energy - depending on the type of exercise you take, you could be improving your muscle strength and stamina levels.
4. Regular exercise can help you to sleep more soundly - just avoid exercising before you go to bed otherwise you will find it difficult to fall asleep.
5. When you exercise with friends it can be a fun way of keeping fit and building your relationships.
6. Regular exercise can also put the energy and sparkle back into the bedroom!

If the thought of exercising seems too much like hard work, find a sport or activity you enjoy, that you can do with a friend, and something that you can fit into your schedule once or twice a week if possible. When you do something with a friend, then you can support each other when one of you has a bad day.

If your role is mainly based indoors, or at a desk, then finding time to exercise when you are working can be a challenge, particularly if you also have a long commute to work. You are going to have to be creative if you want to incorporate some exercise into your working day.

Start good habits now

All of these topics are important, and worth working on, to develop a healthy life and work style. When you are younger, your body can cope and tends to bounce back more easily from burning the candle at both ends, or eating too many unhealthy meals. As you get older, your body will start to complain! If your body is not functioning properly, then it is more difficult to perform your tasks at work, and strong leaders need to be in tip-top condition. Start good habits now, do not wait until you are signed off work with stress, an ulcer, or a heart attack.

As the Mayonnaise Jar story reminds us:
"Pay attention to the things that are critical to your happiness, play with your children, take care of your health, make time for your friends and go out to dinner with your partner because there will always be time to clean the house and fix the car. Set your priorities and take care of the 'golf balls' first for they are the things that really matter, all the rest is just sand."

Summary

1. Ensure that you make time for the 'golf balls' in your life.
2. The quality of your relationships both inside and outside of work, will impact on how you feel about yourself.
3. Review **Exercise 10.2 - The Balanced Wheel** every six

months to ensure you are spending sufficient time in the areas of your life that are important to you.
4. Surround yourself with radiators and reduce the time you spend with drains, and you will find that you have more energy at home and at work.
5. When you look after yourself first, you will be stronger and more able to look after the other important people in your life.
6. Exercise improves your mood. When you exercise regularly you tend to feel better about yourself and your appearance.
7. Refer to your Relax/Excite/Challenge list weekly, and schedule activities in your diary.
8. And remember... *"No matter how full your life may seem, there's always room for a glass of wine* (or cup of tea) *with a friend."*

AFTERWORD

I do hope that reading this book has inspired you, and given you the boost needed to step up to a leadership role. Or, if you are already a leader, has given you some tools and techniques to make you a stronger and more effective leader. I hope that the case studies have given you food for thought, and perhaps re-assured you that others are also facing similar challenges to your own.

If you skipped through the book without doing the exercises, keep the book handy so that you can dip in and complete one when the need arises for a particular issue. Consider asking a trusted colleague or friend to facilitate your thinking, by posing the questions and recording the responses for you.

Being a manager, team leader, or senior leader can be a lonely place. There are high expectations of you, to manage your team effectively, to make tough decisions and deliver results. It is not a weakness to ask for help, so if you do find yourself struggling, excessively stretched or simply need someone to bounce ideas off, reach out for the support of a mentor or a coach. Surely you would recommend that one of your team do the same thing, if it would help get them back on track, and delivering results?

If you completed the Soft Skills Assessment in Chapter One, return to it now and complete it again to see how the exercises have helped move you forward. If there are still areas that you would like to develop, visit www.crowncoaching.com for more information about our Soft Skills training and coaching programmes.

Enjoy your leadership journey,

Helen Isacke

EXERCISES

Chapter One
1.1 – Soft Skills Assessment	29
1.2 – Your Unique Set of Leadership Values	32
1.3 – Living your Values	36

Chapter Two
2.1 – Blow your own Trumpet	47
2.2 – Changing your Beliefs	56
2.3 – Setting your Intentions	61

Chapter Three
3.1 – Your Personal Brand	73
3.2 – Set your Networking Intention	81

Chapter Four
4.1 – Team History	91
4.2 – Digging Deeper	92
4.3 – Creating your Vision	96

Chapter Five
5.1 – Step into the Boss's Shoes	112
5.2 – Hygiene Factors and Motivation	115
5.3 – Uncover your Core Values	118
5.4 – Risks and Benefits	124

Chapter Six
6.1 – Uncovering Assumptions	135
6.2 – Observing Preferences	144
6.3 – Rapport Building	151
6.4 – Define your Stakeholders	153

Chapter Seven
7.1 – Your Guilt List	162
7.2 – Uncover the Triggers	165
7.3 – Set a Positive 'Anchor'	171
7.4 – Strategies for De-Motivation	178

Chapter Eight
8.1 – Creating the Future	189
8.2 – Avoidance Themes	193
8.3 – Courage, and the Pros and Cons	193
8.4 – Problem-Solving Questions	202

Chapter Nine
9.1 – Prioritising your 'To Do' List	215
9.2 – The Five D's	216
9.3 – Delegation Barriers	226
9.4 – Learning to Say NO	230
9.5 – Motivation Magic	233

Chapter Ten
10.1 – The Consequences	240
10.2 – The Balanced Wheel	243
10.3 – Time for Personal Relationships	246
10.4 – Relax/Excite/Challenge	248

TOP TIPS

Chapter Two
Increase your Self-Confidence　　　　　　　　　51

Chapter Three
Expand your Influence　　　　　　　　　　　　74
Effective Networking　　　　　　　　　　　　　82

Chapter Six
Listen with your Heart　　　　　　　　　　　　150

Chapter Seven
Build your Emotional Resilience　　　　　　　　177

Chapter Eight
Handling Difficult People　　　　　　　　　　　195
Dealing with Conflict　　　　　　　　　　　　　198
Coaching Questions　　　　　　　　　　　　　205

Chapter Nine
Tackle Procrastination　　　　　　　　　　　　218
Manage Perfectionism　　　　　　　　　　　　220
Minimise Telephone Interruptions　　　　　　　222
Manage your Inbox　　　　　　　　　　　　　224

RECOMMENDED READING

Eat that Frog, Brian Tracy, Hodder Paperbacks, 2013

Enemies & Advocates, Colin Gautrey, The Gautrey Group, 2011

Gung Ho! How to motivate people in any organisation, Ken Blanchard and Sheldon Bowles, Harper, 2011

How to Talk to Anyone, Neil Lowndes, Thorsons, 2008

Emotional Intelligence: Why it can matter more than IQ, Daniel Goleman, Bloomsbury Publishing plc, 1996

Fierce Conversations, Susan Scott, Piatkus, 2003

Mindfulness, a practical guide to finding peace in a frantic world, Mark Williams & Danny Penman, Piatkus, 2011

Persuasion & Influence for Dummies, Elizabeth Kunkhe, John Wiley & Sons, 2011

Seven Habits of Highly Effective People, Stephen Covey, Simon & Schuster Ltd, 2004

Six Pillars of Self-Esteem, Nathaniel Branden, Bantam Trade 2004
The Human Element, Will Schutz, Jossey Bass 1994

The One Minute Manager meets the Monkey, Ken Blanchard, William Oncken and Hal Burrows, Harper, 2011

Time to Think, Listening to Ignite the Human Mind, Nancy Kline, Cassell Illustrated, 1998

ACKNOWLEDGEMENTS

Thank you to my wonderful family, friends, and networking colleagues, who have been a constant source of support and encouragement.

Huge thanks to Mum, Jane and Chloe for your constant encouragement and Lynne for your careful attention to detail in proof-reading. Thank you Howard for keeping me smiling, and giving me the work life balance I had forgotten was possible. Many thanks to Maureen Atkins, Lee Farnsworth and Romilla Ready, who read the first draft, thank you for the constructive feedback that enabled me to produce what you see here today. Thank you to Jenny Allman, who inadvertently helped me to structure the book as it now is.

Thank you to my clients, who, over the last ten years have shared with me their challenges and aspirations. Your stories have inspired me to write this book, and to help others learn from your experiences. It has been a privilege working with each of you. Thanks to Matt Wright for your patience and editing suggestions, and to Roger Leboff for bringing a smile with your delightful cartoons.

And the biggest thanks of all must go to my daughter Emily, who graduated with a First in Graphic Design, and came home from university at exactly the right time. Thank you Emily, for designing the content, the fabulous cover, and for your patience and determination to produce a comprehensive index when I was ready to give up. I will be forever grateful to you for turning my manuscript into the book I am now so proud of.

ABOUT THE AUTHOR

Helen Isacke spent the first twelve years of her career in the hotel industry, working in front office management and HR. When her two daughters were young, she set up a recruitment agency for nannies, working from home so that she could spend as much time as possible with her girls. Helen succeeded in building an excellent reputation over the following six years, and in 1999, sold the agency. She took on a new position of Marketing Manager, using the skills she had previously developed to promote and grow her own business.

In 2003, Helen was still searching for a role that would utilise her interpersonal skills, and would truly motivate and inspire her. A friend recommended that she find a 'Career Coach'. As Helen searched the internet for a coach, she found herself immersed in articles and websites about coaching, and realised that this was exactly what she wanted to do for a career. She signed up to train as a coach, and found her true passion in life.

Helen is now a highly respected Accredited Coach, NLP Master Practitioner, trainer, and writer. Since 2004, she has been working with managers and leaders to develop their authentic leadership style. She is passionate about helping aspiring and new leaders to enhance the soft skills needed, to manage and motivate themselves, and their teams.

Helen delivers coaching and training in a challenging, supportive and solution focused manner, whilst creating the space for reflection, and growth. She uses a selection of psychometric profiling tools to raise awareness of personality style, behaviour and interaction with others.

Helen set up her company, Crown Coaching Ltd, Marlow, Bucks, UK in 2004. She has a small portfolio of high calibre associates, to help deliver a range of performance development solutions.

You can contact Helen via her website www.crowncoaching.com

INDEX

A

achievement 50
  achievement drive 25
acting as if 76
adaptability 25
anchor 170–172
anger 63, 163
anxiety
  letting go of 166
  triggers 165
appearance 68, 69, 77–79, 188, 191
approval 49, 220
assumptions 58–59, 77, 109, 134, 134–136, 167
attitude 23, 26, 102, 116, 177, 179
attractive 72
authenticity 28–29, 32, 35, 36, 95
authentic leadership 28
avoidance 193

B

balance. *See* Chapter Ten p. 237
balanced wheel 243
baseline state 169, 169–170
behaviour
  defensive 139
beliefs 23, 28, 44, 52–53, 117, 122–123, 135, 138, 167, 220, 226, 234
  changing 56–57
  empowering 44, 53, 55, 57, 84, 138, 168
  limiting 55–57
blame culture 176
Blanchard, Ken 101, 231
blocks
  to better relationships 132
body language 74–75, 146, 149–151, 200

boundaries 94–95, 182
Bowles, Sheldon 101
Branded, Nathaniel 51
Burrows, Hal 231

C

change curve 207–210
character 23, 29, 39–41
clutter 231
coaching
  GROW model 204
  questions 205
  skills 209–210
  style 203–205
collaboration 101
commitment 25, 100, 117
communicating
  values 95
communication 23, 38, 75, 92, 99, 103
  non-verbal 75, 77
  verbal 75
community 101
company objectives 96
comparisons 136
competence 39, 138
confidence 44, 44–45, 49, 76, 166, 192, 196, 232. *See also* self-confidence
conflict 108, 181, 188, 198–201
connections 130–131
control 53, 137–139, 163, 188, 196–200. *See also* self-control
courage 29, 30, 34, 96, 193–194
Covey, Stephen 217
credibility 70–71

D

Day to Day Challenges. *See* Part

Three p. 157
decision-making 69, 84, 101, 214
decisions 34, 35, 38, 39–41, 117, 137, 138, 139, 161, 175, 194, 214
defensive behaviour 139
delegation 225–227, 241
de-motivation 177–179
  causes 178
  strategies 178–179
difficult conversations 192
difficult meetings 188–191
difficult people 175, 195
difficult situations 169, 175, 188–189. *See* Chapter Eight p. 187
DISC profiling 40
disorganisation 218
distractions 178, 221, 225

E

e-mail 223–224
emotional feelings 160–168
emotional intelligence 24–26
emotional resilience 175–176, 177, 179
emotions 143, 161–170, 175–176
  exploring. *See* Chapter Seven p. 159
  negative 161–167, 172–174, 181
  other people 182–184
  positive 161, 169–172
empathy 24, 26
employee engagement 25, 100–101
employee satisfaction 100
employee surveys 114–115
energy 39, 102–103
engaging your team 100–101. *See* Chapter Four p. 89
enthusiasm 102–103, 245
Erikkson, Milton 195
exercise 251–252

expectations 35, 94
  client 114–115
  managing 108, 108–109, 114, 199
  mutual 108
  self-imposed 108, 125–126
  setting 181. *See* Chapter Five p. 107
  team 113–114
  unrealistic 123–124
extraversion 39
eye contact 75, 76, 149, 150, 200

F

failure 63, 176–177, 218
fear 160, 166–167, 172, 206
  being humiliated 138, 168
  being ignored 138
  being rejected 138
  deep-seated 124, 133, 138, 182
  failure 218
  making mistakes 208
  of being found out 139, 166–168
  the common cause 193
  unknown 208, 209
feedback 38, 63, 103, 115, 130, 199, 200
  avoid giving 199
  constructive 36, 199, 200
  difficult 95, 103
  positive 196, 200
feelings
  emotional 160, 167–168
  intuitive 160
  negative 63
  paying attention to 35
  physiological 160
  positive 76, 138, 170, 192
FIRO theory 136–138
First 100 days. *See* Part Two p. 87
five D's 216

flight or fight 163, 165, 167
foundations
  setting the. *See* Chapter One p. 21
friends 130, 239, 246
  keeping your 94–95
frustration 63, 84, 111, 118, 126, 164, 172, 196, 209, 228
future
  creating the 189–190

G

Gautrey, Colin 153
getting organised 223, 231–232
goals 50, 90, 108, 116, 217–218
  achieve your 25
  long-term 217
  PRISM 96
  short-term 217
  SMART 99
  unrealistic 219
Goleman, Daniel 24
grooming 77–79
GROW model 204–205
guilt 60, 161, 162–163, 172, 196

H

hard skills 23
healthy eating 250–251
hygiene factors 115–116

I

inadequate 167–168
inbox 223–224
inclusion 137–138, 140
in control 172, 189
influence 23, 24, 68–69, 73–74, 137–139, 152
initiative 25
inner critic 53
inner dialogue 45, 80
innovation 25, 30

insights 40
Institute of Employment Studies 100
integrity 25, 29, 30, 103
intentions 60–63
internal clients 114
internal state 178, 196
interruptions 214, 221–222, 225
introversion 39
intuition 25, 39, 149

J

judging 40
Jung, Carl 39

K

key influencers 91
Kübler-Ross 207–210
Kuhnke, Elizabeth 74

L

language patterns 143
leadership 22
  authentic 28–29
  personality 38
  preparing for. *See* Part One p. 19
  style 28–29, 38, 94
  values 29–30, 32–33, 34, 44, 98
leveraging diversity 26
likeability 138
listening skills 149–150, 182
Lowndes, Leil 82

M

managing change 206–207
managing your mindset 52–53
matching 145–147, 200
  words 147–148
mayonnaise jar 238–239
meetings 113, 228
  difficult 188–190

preparing for 191-192
mentally absent 245
Meyer, John 24
micro-manage 138, 139
milestones 99-100, 108, 217-218
mind-reading 58-59, 84, 133, 193
mindset 76, 90, 232
    managing your 52-53, 60, 245. *See* Chapter Two p. 43
    positive 62-63
mirroring 146-148, 200
mission 95, 114
mistakes 63, 192, 208
motivation 25, 132, 173, 177-179, 214, 232-233, 250
Myers Briggs (MBTI) 39

N

networking 79-82

O

Oncken, William 231
openness 93, 137
optimism 25

P

panic 173
passion 95-96, 98
perceiving 40
perfectionism 174, 219-221, 227, 241
performance review 189, 192, 204
personal brand 68-71, 73
    developing your. *See* Chapter Three p. 67
personal impact 72, 75, 84-85
personality 23, 29, 38-41
personality profiling 38-41
personality type 39-41, 58, 207
personal relationships 244-245, 246-247

persuasion 73-74
physical well-being 250-252
physiological feelings 160
physiology 76-77, 84
political awareness 26
positive impact 69, 79, 188
predecessor 113, 133, 136
preferences 25, 39, 144
    auditory 142-148
    kinaesthetic 142, 143-148
    visual 142-148
preparing
    for leadership. *See* Part One p. 19
presence 68
presentations 55, 219
prioritising 214-216
PRISM goals 96-97
problem-solving 38, 201-202
procrastination 218-219
purpose
    sense of 29, 34, 47, 96, 98, 116

Q

questions
    well-formed 97

R

rapport 145-152
reflect, time to 50
rejection 175, 176
relationships
    managing 26. *See* Chapter Six p. 129
relax 247-248
representational systems 142-143
    auditory 142
    kinaesthetic 143
    visual 142
reputation 68, 74, 103
responsibility 25, 36, 117, 137, 192, 227

role model 34, 36, 72, 102–103, 232

S

Salovey, Peter 24
saying no 229–231
Schutz, Will 136, 140
self-acceptance 48–49
self-awareness 24–25, 38, 60, 122
self-confidence 25, 51
self-control 25
self-doubt 44, 50
self-esteem 44, 44–46, 45–47, 49, 139
self-promotion 71
self-regard 49
self-respect 29, 136, 188
self-talk 83
self-worth 25, 29
sensing 26
sensory
  phrases 148
  words 148
significant 138
SMART goals 99
soft skills 13–16, 22–24
stakeholders 114, 152–153
strengths 25, 38, 48
stress 172–175
  causes of 174
stress curve 173
support network 246–247

T

targets 103, 113, 123–124
TDI 39–41
team
  engaging your new. *See* Chapter Four p. 89
teamwork 101
tears 183–184
telephone 222–223
thinking 39–40, 41, 52–53, 58, 160

thoughts
  controlling 53
time
  management. *See* Chapter Nine p. 213
tone 75, 143, 146, 147
transparency 29, 35
trust 44–45, 74, 101, 130, 145
trustworthiness 25
type theory 40–41

U

unconscious
  assumptions 58–59, 68, 75
  behaviour 35
  expectations 122
  mind 62
  thoughts 52
uncovering assumptions 135–136
unrealistic expectations 174

V

values 28, 29, 84, 117
  communicating 35
  conflicting 30–31, 118
  core 114, 117, 118–122
  leadership 32–33, 34, 44, 98
  personal 95
vision
  commuicating your 98–99
  creating your 96–98

W

well-being 92, 101, 250
workaholic 238
work-life balance 240–244